P9-DIH-513

100 DOGS WHO CHANGED CIVILIZATION

HISTORY'S MOST INFLUENTIAL CANINES

BY SAM STALL

QUIRK BOOKS
PHILADELPHIA

To Cortney the corgi, my greatest admirer.
The feeling was mutual.

CONTENTS

INTRODUCTION

"Histories are more full of the examples of the fidelity of dogs than of friends."
—Alexander Pope

Humanity's long, fruitful, extremely complex relationship with canines began strictly as a business deal. It probably went something like this: Tens of thousands of years ago, for reasons unknown, a pack of wolves joined forces with a group of cavemen. This intermingling created what modern business executives call synergy. The wolves possessed keen senses, speed, and strength. The humans possessed freakishly big brains and wielded deadly weapons.

Nature's odd couple proved an unbeatable combination. But on the way to global dominance, something strange happened. The wolves turned into dogs—domesticated canines physically and emotionally tailored to meet specific human needs. We still hunted together, but we also herded, toiled, and even marched off to war side by side. And somewhere along the line, humans stopped seeing dogs as mere tools. They regarded them as colleagues, confidants, and friends. Even, dare we say, as man's best friend.

The feeling, apparently, is mutual. Of course there's no telling exactly how dogs regard us, because they can't speak for themselves. One can only judge them by their actions. Actions that, over the centuries, have included displays of devotion, courage, and selflessness that put the deeds of many human heroes to shame—and made a book such as this not only possible, but plausible.

What have canines done? They have rescued some of us from eminent death. They've saved even more of us from boredom and loneliness. Their presence has been a stirring example on the battlefield and a comfort in the home.

The average dog performs acts of everyday heroism far from the spotlight, but some have become deservedly famous for their deeds. One can say without exaggeration that the fates of nations and empires have sometimes rested in capable canine paws. Alexander the Great lived long enough to earn his title only because his war dog, Peritas, saved his life in battle (page 166). Napoleon would never have met his Waterloo had a fisherman's dog not rescued him from drowning (page 67). And William the Silent, father of the Dutch nation and ancestor of King William III of England, would have been slain in his bed by assassins without his pug's timely warning (page 65).

Other great canines left their marks in more unexpected but equally remarkable ways. Movies ranging from *Casablanca* to *The Matrix* might never have been made had a German shepherd named Rin Tin Tin not singlehandedly saved Warner Bros. Studios from bankruptcy (page 115). The English poet Alexander Pope would have been struck down in midcareer had it not been for his Great Dane, Bounce (page 94). And the operas of Richard Wagner might have turned out very differently without the artistic input of his furry collaborators, Peps and Fips (page 96).

Dogs figure prominently in many of humanity's most remarkable political, cultural, and artistic endeavors, and their influence is almost always for the good. But that shouldn't surprise us, because almost every dog, whether he changes history or not, positively influences the harassed humans around him. In exchange for a pat on the head, we get unstinting devotion. In exchange for a bowl of food, we gain an unflinching ally. In exchange for a spot by the hearth, we get a lifetime's worth of love. It's been a profitable relationship for both of us. But humans definitely got the better part of the deal.

We know deep down that we're unworthy of such a friend. But maybe, just maybe, dogs can inspire us to be more like the people they *think* we are.

SCIENCE
AND
NATURE

SNUPPY

THE WORLD'S FIRST CLONED DOG

Dog fanciers like to think that every canine is unique. But that can't be said for Snuppy, the world's first cloned dog.

Born on April 24, 2005, Snuppy was the product of years of work by scientists at South Korea's Seoul National University (SNU)—the name *Snuppy* is a fusion of *SNU* and *puppy*. In order to produce this single clone, researchers transferred more than one thousand dog embryos into 123 female canines. This produced a paltry three pregnancies, only one of which proved successful. Snuppy, an Afghan hound created from an ear cell belonging to another hound named Tai, was carried to term by a yellow Labrador retriever.

One might wonder why they bothered. The scientists said it was because such clones could be used to study human diseases, or perhaps to produce human-compatible stem cells. The man in charge of the project, Hwang Woo-suk, was soon to be discredited by revelations that he'd faked research on the cloning of human stem cells. But while Hwang fibbed about his work with humans, follow-up studies proved that his claims about Snuppy were all true.

LAIKA

THE FIRST EARTHLING IN SPACE

After more than half a century of space exploration, many people forget that the first creature to reach orbit was canine rather than human. The dog who opened the high frontier was a tiny stray from the streets of Moscow named Laika.

Her flight was a high-tech publicity stunt, designed to spotlight the Soviet Union's lead in rocketry. Soviet premier Nikita Khrushchev informed the Russian scientists responsible for the space-race–inaugurating *Sputnik* satellite that he wanted a new ship launched on November 7, 1957, to mark the fortieth anniversary of the communist revolution. Though the scientists weren't yet ready to launch the new, more sophisticated vehicle they'd been developing, saying "no" wasn't an option. So they cobbled together another space ship in about a month. The rough-and-ready craft contained rudimentary life-support systems so it could carry a living organism into space, but time didn't permit the development of a heat shield and parachute system that would allow for that passenger's safe return. Whoever rode the ship, designated *Sputnik II*, would make a one-way trip.

The unfortunate space pioneer was picked from a pack of Moscow street mutts rounded up and trained for experimental flights. Dogs were the selected species because the scientists believed they possessed the intelligence and discipline to cope with space travel, along with the ability to handle long periods in confined spaces. The first flight was "awarded" to a female husky mix who weighed about thirteen pounds (6 kg)—perfect for the satellite's cramped quarters. At first called Kudryavka (Little Curly), her name was later changed to Laika (Barker) when her original moniker proved too tricky for members of the international media to spell or pronounce. In America, she came to be known as Muttnik.

Sputnik II was launched with Laika on board on November 3, 1957, in a worldwide blaze of publicity. Placing the first living being in orbit was trumpeted by the Soviets as a major achievement. However, in later years it was revealed to be not quite as groundbreaking as originally portrayed.

For decades the Russians claimed that Laika survived for days in orbit before finally succumbing to a malfunction in her life-support system. The truth wasn't revealed until forty-five years after her historic flight. In 2002, Russian scientists who had worked on the program admitted that the poor dog had died only hours into the mission, probably from fright. Her capsule remained in orbit until April 14, 1958, when it reentered the atmosphere and burned up.

Thankfully, of the thirteen Russian space dogs sent into orbit over the ensuing decade, Laika was the only one who couldn't be retrieved. But in the eyes of dog owners worldwide, that was one too many. "The more time passes, the more I'm sorry about it," said Soviet-era rocket scientist Oleg Gazenko decades after the project. "We did not learn enough from this mission to justify the death of the dog."

It's some small consolation that today Laika is lionized for her sacrifice. She's been featured in endless books and movies and emblazoned on postage stamps around the world. But perhaps the most fitting testament is her place on Moscow's gigantic Monument to the Conquerors of Space. In the spirit of collectivism, the massive bas-relief at its base contains no images of specific cosmo-

nauts or scientists involved in the program. The only explorer who earned a personal portrait is Laika, shown inside the capsule that would become her final resting place.

DUMPY

THE HOMELESS MUTT WHO BECAME A PUREBRED

Purebred dogs are considered the aristocracy of the canine world. But just as with human nobility, some of the most vaunted names arise from humble beginnings.

It's hard to imagine a humbler start than that of the Boykin spaniel, a medium-sized hunting dog that's widely known in the American South. Incredibly, the breed can be traced back to a single stray who went by the not-very-aristocratic name of Dumpy. Alexander L. White found the poor, bedraggled creature in 1911, loitering outside a church in Spartanburg, South Carolina. White took him home, fed and bathed him, and discovered during numerous hunting trips that Dumpy had the makings of an excellent retriever. His friend, dog trainer Whit Boykin, was likewise impressed. White turned the churchyard refugee over to Boykin, who crossed him with other promising hunting dogs.

Eventually, after much fine-tuning, Dumpy's progeny became the elegant-looking Boykin spaniels seen at dog shows today. The Boykin is even recognized as the state dog of South Carolina—quite a step up for the sons and daughters of a stray mutt.

TITINA

THE FIRST DOG TO FLY OVER THE NORTH POLE

Almost every dog who has ever visited the earth's arctic regions did so while pulling a sled. But that's not the case for an intrepid fox terrier named Titina. She arrived at the North Pole in relative comfort aboard an airship.

The little dog started life as a starving stray on the streets of Rome. But one night in 1925, she had the good fortune of running into Italian dirigible pioneer Umberto Nobile. From then on, Nobile and Titina (she was named after an Italian song) were inseparable. They shared danger, adventure, and, finally, disgrace.

The two were so close that in 1926 Nobile made the unusual, even ill-advised, decision to take his ten-pound (5 kg) mascot with him on a historic attempt to fly an airship of his own design over the North Pole. The tiny Titina didn't take up much space, but as the expedition's commander, the famed Norwegian explorer Roald Amundsen, pointed out in the most blunt and angry terms, conditions were so cramped on board that the sixteen-man crew of the airship *Norge* didn't even have space to sit down. The only individual who enjoyed that luxury was Titina, who nested on a pile of supplies.

Her trip over the pole made the diminutive dog a media darling. Dispatches from the expedition detailed everything from her living conditions to what she wore (a red woolen jersey). Her biography even appeared in the *New York Times*. After the flight she went on a world tour with Nobile, meeting everyone from Rudolph Valentino to Benito Mussolini. The great airman so loved his dog that he wouldn't allow his picture to be taken without her.

But Titina was destined to share Nobile's bad times as well. On May 25, 1928, during another polar expedition, Nobile's airship *Italia* crashed in the midst of a storm, killing several crew members. The small group of survivors, including Nobile and Titina, salvaged what they could from the wreck and hunkered down on the ice, awaiting rescue.

A month passed before the party was found by a Swedish search plane. It was then that Nobile made the decision that destroyed his reputation. Told that the pilot had been ordered to pick up no one but him, he boarded the plane with his dog and left the rest of his crew behind. As fate would have it, the aircraft crashed when it attempted a second rescue run. The remaining survivors, some of them badly wounded, had to spend many additional weeks on the ice before they were picked up.

Nobile was excoriated by the press for his actions, particularly in Italy, where his success—and his open feuds with the Fascist government—

had made him many enemies in Mussolini's regime. Wrecking the *Italia* and killing so many of his crew seemed bad enough, but abandoning them on the ice, no matter what he'd been told by the pilot of the rescue plane, was even worse. And choosing to take his dog added the final, aggravating exclamation point.

The man who conquered the pole by air was thoroughly disgraced. But there was some consolation, at least. He would outlive Mussolini, and see his name cleared—at least officially—of any misdoing by a 1945 Italian Air Force inquiry. He was even returned to the rank of major general. And, of course, even in his darkest days, he never lost the love and solace of Titina. From the bitter cold arctic to the bitterness of public disrepute, she never left his side.

ROBOT

THE DOG WHO DISCOVERED SOME OF THE WORLD'S FIRST WORKS OF ART

One of the world's greatest cultural treasures is, quite literally, located in a hole in the ground. And it might have remained there, undiscovered, to this very day, were it not for the timely misstep of one French dog.

It happened near the village of Montignac, France. On September 12, 1940, four boys were out searching for treasure allegedly buried in a secret tunnel in the surrounding countryside. The kids had no luck, but their dog, Robot, did. He discovered (some accounts say he fell into and had to be rescued from) a dark hole that his human companions were sure led to untold riches.

They had no idea how right they were. It was the entrance to the now world-famous Cave of Lascaux, an underground complex filled with beautiful and nearly pristine cave paintings, all of them more—perhaps much more—than ten thousand years old. Ironically, Robot's discovery was almost destroyed by the attention it received. The heat and high humidity created by thousands of daily visitors started to damage the cave paintings, and Lascaux had to be closed to the public in 1963.

JO-FI

THE DOG WHO HELPED SIGMUND FREUD SIZE UP HIS PATIENTS

Sigmund Freud, the father of psychotherapy, was a card-carrying dog person. He loved them so much that in later years, on his birthday, his daughter Anna would dress up the family pets in party hats. They had their own chairs at the table and would celebrate and partake of birthday cake alongside the human members of Freud's clan.

He had a particular fondness for chow chows, of which he owned several. Of these, the most important was Jo-Fi. The great psychoanalyst believed dogs were excellent judges of character and that they helped put people at ease. For this reason, he allowed Jo-Fi to sit in on patient interviews. If someone was calm and at peace, the dog would lie down relatively near him or her; if someone was full of hidden tension, Jo-Fi would keep his distance.

But that wasn't the dog's only, or even most useful, talent. Jo-Fi could also unerringly tell when a session was up. After fifty minutes had passed, the big chow would get up, stretch, and head for the office door. Thus Freud always knew, without crassly glancing at his watch, when it was time to usher a patient out the door.

GEORGE

THE DOG WHO COULD SMELL CANCER

Even with the help of the priciest, most advanced medical equipment, detecting cancer in its early stages can be difficult—unless you happen to be a dog. Scientists have discovered that when it comes to finding some forms of this deadly disease, a sensitive, well-trained nose may work better than the highest of high technology.

The idea of dogs sniffing out tumors as if they were rabbits seems absurd. How can a canine, no matter how finely tuned its sense of smell, accomplish something so difficult? But in 1989, the British medical journal *The Lancet* printed an anecdotal report about a British mutt who developed an obsessive interest in a mole on her owner's thigh. The dog's unnerved master had the blemish checked out and discovered it was a malignant melanoma—a melanoma that would have eventually killed her, had it not been found.

That account, along with a handful of similar stories, piqued the interest of American dermatologist and skin cancer specialist Dr. Armand Cognetta of Tallahassee, Florida. Realizing that many melanoma cases go unreported until it's too late to save the patient, he wondered if dogs could be trained to sniff out the disease in its beginning stages. But how does one train a cancer dog? Unsure of how to proceed, he contacted Duane Pickel, the former head of the Tallahassee Police canine corps, and asked if he knew of a four-legged candidate who was up for such a challenge. Pickel nominated his own pet, a standard schnauzer named George.

George was already a highly skilled bomb-sniffing dog. However, his new assignment required even more rigorous preparation. First, he was taught to sniff out concealed test tubes containing tiny bits of malignant melanomas. Then a sample was bandaged to a volunteer, along with numerous other bandages concealing nothing. During dozens of trials, George accumulated a 97 percent detection rate. Finally, he was unleashed on a handful of actual skin cancer patients. The schnauzer managed to "diagnose" six out of seven.

The idea of a dog "sniffing out" cancer really isn't that much of a stretch. They're certainly equipped for it. Canines possess more than 200 million smell-sensing cells in their noses (compared to a human's relatively paltry 5 million), and they've proven themselves capable of locating other extremely challenging targets, from a small cache of illicit drugs in the huge hold of a ship to a single pheasant in a vast field. And since the human track record of finding melanomas in their earliest phases is abysmal, any help dogs can offer would be providential—not to mention much cheaper and easier to do than almost any conventional medical test.

George, who showed the possibilities of such a technique, passed away in 2002 from a brain tumor. But the work continues. Several new studies have been conducted, including a British attempt to teach dogs to detect bladder cancer by smelling patients' urine. Amazingly, one of the supposedly healthy people who was used as part of the experiment's "control" group was found to have a very early case of bladder cancer when the dogs reacted strongly to his supposedly normal pee. Thanks to their sensitive noses, he was treated and recovered. He became one of the first—but not the last—cancer patients to owe his health to a dog.

THE BROWN DOG

THE UNKNOWN MUTT WHOSE DEATH FURTHERED THE CAUSE OF ANIMAL RIGHTS

Not all dogs who contribute to the advancement of the human race do so voluntarily. Hundreds of thousands of canines have died in laboratories, subjected to everything from dangerous experiments to vivisections. For a long time, no one thought much about it—until the lonely death of a single nameless stray triggered a public outcry.

In February 1903, the dog in question—a small terrier known to history as the Brown Dog—was killed after being subjected to vivisection at the Department of Physiology at University College London. Sadly, there was nothing unusual about the macabre affair. It happened regularly for the edification of the students. But this case was different. Two of the witnesses that day were Leisa Schartau and Louise Lind-af-Hageby, Swedish anti-vivisectionists who had enrolled at the London School of Medicine for Women specifically to witness and record such procedures. They presented their notes to Stephen Coleridge, the honorary secretary of Great Britain's Anti-Vivisection Society, who publicly accused the doctor responsible for the Brown Dog of not properly anesthetizing him, as the law required, and of using the animal for more than one experiment, which was also illegal.

The doctor promptly sued Coleridge for libel, but though he won the legal case, he lost in the court of public opinion. A furious uproar over the dog's treatment erupted in the press, with one tabloid raising £5,735 to pay Coleridge's court fine. Things really heated up when a monument to Brown Dog was raised in London. Unveiled on September 15, 1906, it was an innocuous-looking water fountain with a bronze dog on top and an incendiary inscription dedicating it, "In Memory of the Brown Terrier Dog done to Death in the Laboratories of University College in February 1903 . . . [after] . . . having been handed from one Vivisector to another till Death came to his Release."

Large-scale riots ensued as London medical students, bent on defacing the monument, fought running battles with neighborhood toughs. The statue was finally removed in 1910 and, it is presumed, destroyed. But the Brown Dog, and what he represented, wasn't forgotten. In 1985 a new statue was unveiled in the London neighborhood of Battersea, bearing the same searing indictment of animal experimentation. But this time, no one came to the practice's defense.

CAP

THE SHEPHERD'S DOG WHO STEERED FLORENCE NIGHTINGALE INTO NURSING

One can't overestimate the importance of Florence Nightingale to the medical profession. Born in 1820, the daughter of rich, upper-crust English parents, Nightingale was expected to become an obedient wife, tucked away in a country manor. Instead, she chose a life of service by becoming a nurse, one of the era's most reviled professions. And no wonder. At the time, the typical "nurse" was an ill-trained orderly with little more medical knowledge than a scullery maid.

But Nightingale changed all that. She studied well-run hospitals throughout Europe and became a crusader for a then-revolutionary concept: namely, that a clean, well-organized infirmary staffed by knowledgeable, sympathetic caregivers was better than a dirty, disorganized one staffed by callous, incompetent boobs—which pretty much summed up the typical facility of her era.

She became an international celebrity during the Crimean War, in which Great Britain, France, and the Ottoman Empire battled Russia for control of the Crimean Peninsula. Military hospital conditions were such a scandal that Nightingale, along with a small corps of volunteer nurses, was dispatched by Britain's secretary of war to see what could be done. By a Herculean effort, she organized the relief program so efficiently that the hospital death rate sank from 42 percent to 2 percent. Nightingale returned home a national hero and used her fame to work tirelessly for hospital reform until her death in 1910.

What inspired her all-consuming interest in helping others? Perhaps it was an incident that took place in 1837, when Nightingale was only seventeen years old. One day, an old shepherd informed her that his dog, Cap, had been severely injured when some boys threw stones at him. One rock seemingly broke his leg, which meant he couldn't herd sheep. The shepherd couldn't afford to keep a lame dog, so he planned to kill Cap that evening.

Nightingale, appalled, asked permission to visit the dog. She and a companion discovered that his leg was severely bruised, but not broken, and carefully bandaged it. A few days later, Cap was his old self.

Soon thereafter Nightingale dreamed that God was calling her to devote her life to medicine. And the young girl, more than a little inspired by her work with Cap, heeded the call.

BOTHIE

THE ONLY DOG TO VISIT THE NORTH AND SOUTH POLES

Plenty of canines have pulled sleds through the Arctic and Antarctic, but one intrepid dog, a wiry Jack Russell terrier named Bothie, got to visit both the top and the bottom of the world without ever even laying eyes on a sled.

The little dog belonged to famed British explorer Sir Ranulph Fiennes and his wife, Virginia. He was acquired in 1977, two years before the couple left on the Transglobe Expedition to circumnavigate the planet via the poles, a trek they had planned for the better part of a decade. By aircraft and ship, they would travel around the world from pole to pole, first visiting Antarctica, then finishing up at the Arctic.

Bothie couldn't go on the first leg of the expedition, which cut through Africa. The threat of disease and the extreme heat were considered too much for him. But once the group took to the seas on their own ship, the little terrier was flown in, equipped with his own harness to tether him to the deck during rough weather. He was also spared the long overland trek to the heart of Antarctica. Once the expedition reached that goal in January 1980, he was brought in by plane and furnished with

cold-weather gear that included special caps, booties, and body stockings.

Many months later, Bothie completed the feat at the North Pole. It was the crowning moment of the Transglobe Expedition, which began in 1979 and concluded on August 29, 1982. Not surprisingly, Bothie became a celebrity. He was voted Great Britain's Pet of the Year in 1982, and in 1983 he was allowed to do a circuit of honor in the show ring at Crufts, the world's most prestigious dog show. But perhaps even better, Bothie found a girlfriend during his adventures. While in the Yukon he met an enormous Newfoundland-husky-Labrador cross who was named Black Dog by her human associates. The two spent the rest of the trip together, and, after being parted for several months in mandatory quarantine once they got to Great Britain, remained a couple thereafter.

JET

THE DOG WHO BECAME AN AIR TRAFFIC CONTROLLER

The threat of midair collisions with birds is an ever-present danger at airports around the world. In the United States alone, roughly 2,500 such bird strikes take place annually. These close encounters are almost universally deadly to the foul, and they're no picnic for human pilots, either. A midair run-in can shatter a jetliner's cockpit windows or cause a catastrophic loss of thrust if the avian victim is sucked into an engine.

That's why airports spend a great deal of time and money trying to keep crows, geese, and other potential flight hazards from nesting around their runways. Over the years, airports have used everything from firecrackers to smoke bombs to trained falcons. All of these remedies proved expensive, complicated, and not very effective. But in 1999, Southwest Florida International Airport became the first major airport to deploy what has become the most technically advanced, highly effective answer to the problem—a dog named Jet.

The two-year-old border collie turned out to be an excellent solution. After extensive training he was sent out with airport personnel to patrol the grounds. Whenever flocks picked roosting spots that were too close to air traffic corridors, Jet would "encourage" them to leave by charging in unannounced, putting them to flight. His herding-dog background was a key advantage. Jet could be counted on to drive off the birds without harming them. And because his movements are so similar to those of stalking foxes or coyotes, the birds never became blasé about his presence, the way they so often did with other deterrents such as firecrackers and smoke bombs.

In 1998, the year before Jet arrived, there were sixteen bird strikes at the airport. During his first year on the job, the number dropped to four, and it remained in the single digits thereafter. The program proved so effective that a new border collie named Radar was recruited to replace Jet when he retired in 2001. Other airports have taken note and purchased their own bird-chasing canines. They're currently on duty at Dover Air Force Base and at municipal airports in Augusta, Georgia, and Vancouver, British Columbia, to name a few.

AIBO

THE DOG WHO WAS A ROBOT

Dog breeders spend a great deal of time and energy attempting to "improve" our canine friends through selective breeding. But in the late 1990s the engineers at Sony took matters to the next level. Rather than trying to make traditional dogs better, they built a new one from the ground up—a dog that doesn't need walks, won't wet the carpet, or chew on the furniture. All this new breed required was a hard drive and quiet place to recharge its battery.

Their brainchild was named AIBO (short, sort of, for Artificial Intelligence Robot). The four-legged, chrome-plated contraption was the first commercially produced, autonomous robotic dog. It could do pretty much everything real canines can do, plus plenty of things they can't. Thanks to their sophisticated programming, early versions could putter around the house on their own initiative, recognize human faces, and understand and respond to dozens of voice commands. They could even be programmed to start their existence in "puppy mode," then slowly develop into adult dogs equipped with unique personalities constructed from their "life" experiences.

Later versions of the robot could do considerably more. Among its many other talents, the model ERS-743 can speak more than 1,000 English words; understand a smattering of Spanish; dance along with music; and connect to the Internet and recite news and sports feeds for its owner—all for about $2,100.

The little machines were undeniably fun, but they were a bit too pricey for the average dog and/or technology lover. To the dismay of robot canine fans worldwide, Sony announced in 2006 that it planned to pull the plug on AIBO. But the discontinuation of the little dogs may have major repercussions on the development of robotics technology. Building a machine that can walk, see, and communicate is difficult and expensive, so engineers and artificial intelligence experts routinely used the comparatively cheap AIBO as a test bed. The ersatz canine even became a centerpiece at the annual RoboCup autonomous robot soccer competition. AIBOs have their own division in the tournament, in which squads with names such as FU-Fighters and the RoboLog Project face off against other teams of robots from around the world. Given their undeniable utility, hackers may be teaching these old dogs new tricks for years to come.

RICO

THE WORLD'S SMARTEST DOG

Plenty of people think their dogs can understand what they say. Based on groundbreaking studies of a singularly intelligent border collie named Rico, those people may be more correct than they ever imagined.

All border collies are smart, but Rico is, apparently, a doggie rocket scientist. He seems to possess a vocabulary of approximately two hundred words, is able to identify specific toys from his vast collection by their names alone, and has even displayed deductive reasoning.

In 2004, scientists from the Max Planck Institute for Evolutionary Anthropology in Leipzig, Germany, conducted a study of Rico's behavior and later published their results in the journal *Science*. Rico found himself in the lab after his owners claimed that the nine-year-old canine knew the specific names of every one of his dozens and dozens of toys. The scientists decided to test those claims in a series of carefully constructed experiments. First they placed Rico and his owner in one room, with a selection of his toys in another. Rico was then given the name of the specific object to retrieve, and he made the right choice thirty-seven out of forty times. But then came the *really* big news. A selection of the dog's possessions was placed in the room, along with a brand new object Rico had never before seen. His owner then called out the new name and told Rico to go get it. Amazingly, the brilliant border collie deduced that the unfamiliar word applied to the unfamiliar object, and he retrieved it. Child-development experts call this singular skill "fast mapping"—the ability to quickly assign a meaning to a new word. Most had thought the technique, which toddlers use to learn language, was strictly a human trait.

The idea that dogs can possess the ability to fast-map is a scientific bombshell. Assuming the study data hold up to scrutiny, it could mean a couple of things: either that Rico is perhaps the smartest dog in the world, or that (more likely) all dogs possess similar abilities to a greater or lesser degree. The work led some scientists to speculate on matters that many dog owners have long suspected but couldn't voice for fear of ridicule. "If Rico had a human vocal tract, one would presume that he should be able to say the names of the items as well, or at least try to do so," Sue Savage-Rumbaugh, who studies animal communication and intelligence at Georgia State University, told the *Washington Post*. "It also raises the issue of whether Rico and/or other dogs or other mammals might already be trying to say words, but have great difficulty being understood."

Such musings are music to dog owners' ears. Of course, Rico can't use language with as much dexterity as, say, the average human first-grader. So far his talents seem to be limited to matters concerning his toy collection and the fetching of specific objects from it. Presumably, if one asked him whether the moon was a ball, or if a specific stuffed toy made him glad or sad, he'd have nothing to offer.

But perhaps, just perhaps, he might. Work is already under way to see if Rico is as good at grasping abstractions as he is at grabbing toys. Given the surprises this singular pooch has already sprung, there's no telling what might happen.

MISSY

THE DOG WHO HELPED PIONEER THE CLONING OF CATS

Like most people, John Sperling had a soft spot for his dog, a border collie–Siberian husky mix named Missy. And like most people, he dreaded the day when his companion would pass away. But *unlike* most people, Sperling was in a position to do something about it—something that would bring about a novel advance in cloning technology.

Sperling is not just a dog lover, but a *billionaire* dog lover. He built much of his fortune through the University of Phoenix, a for-profit teaching institution he founded in 1976. He also made a name for himself as a biotechnology entrepreneur. In 1991 he bankrolled, to the tune of roughly $4 million, an effort to clone his best friend, Missy. Called the Missyplicity Project, it was a joint venture between Texas A&M University and Bio-Arts and Research Corporation (BARC), an umbrella company for Sperling and another San Francisco–area businessman. The scientists at Texas A&M labored through the late 1990s and early 2000s, implanting embryos infused with Missy's DNA into various "host" females, but none of the pregnancies proved viable.

After years of fruitless labor, the team reached two conclusions. The first was that dogs are very,

very hard to clone. The second, which came almost as an afterthought, was that cats are much easier.

Thus the Missyplicity Project refocused itself. If it couldn't replicate man's best friend, it would settle for his second-best friend. In 2001, after eighty-seven failed attempts, the research group produced CC (short for Copy Cat), the world's first cloned feline. The kitten seemed to point the way to a unique new business—resurrecting dead pets for fun and profit.

To capitalize on the technological breakthrough, a company with the deliciously *Twilight Zone*-ish name of Genetic Savings & Clone was founded to offer bereaved cat owners carbon copies of their dearly departed friends. Those with an eye toward the future could store their cat's DNA in the company's PetBank. Then, when the original feline passed away, they could use the Nine Lives Extravaganza cloning program to create Fluffy 2.0. All it took to see this new version of your cat alive and well again were the services of Genetic Savings & Clone's state-of-the-art Madison, Wisconsin, laboratory—and, of course, a payment of roughly $32,000.

Not surprisingly, animal rights advocates were horrified by the thought of spending a fortune to resurrect dead felines while thousands of perfectly good live ones languished in animal shelters. That, and the steep price for its services, doomed Genetic Savings & Clone to an early demise. After creating a handful of custom cats, the firm closed its doors in 2006.

As it turned out, the high cost wasn't the only problem with cat cloning. Nature, it seems, hates to repeat herself. Though a clone and its donor undeniably carry the same set of genetic instructions, subtle environmental factors can sometimes cause slight—and not-so-slight—variations in physical appearance. This difficulty was first noted in CC, the "original" feline clone. Tests showed that she was indeed an exact genetic copy of her donor, a calico named Rainbow. And yet, as if nature were playing a joke, her fur was a different color.

Canine cloning, which was finally accomplished in a South Korean lab (see page 12), has so far proved too complicated, expensive, and failure-prone for commercial application. As for Missy, she passed away quietly on July 6, 2002. For better or worse, there will never be another dog like her.

OTHER CANINES OF DISTINCTION

VETEROK AND UGOLYOK: Two dogs launched into orbit by the Soviets in 1966, then recovered safely after twenty-two days. Humans wouldn't stay in space that long until 1974's Skylab 2 mission.

DIAMOND: One of many canines owned by Sir Isaac Newton. Diamond gave his master a nervous breakdown when he knocked over a candle on Newton's desk, burning his notes.

POLLY: Charles Darwin's terrier, who slept in a basket near her master's desk. Immortalized by a reference made to her in Darwin's The Expression of the Emotions in Man and Animals.

BUDDY: America's first formally trained guide dog for the blind. Her master, Morris Frank, helped establish Seeing Eye, the first guide dog school in the United States.

SAILOR AND CANTON: Male and female Newfoundlands who, in 1807, were stranded in the United States when the English ship on which they traveled sank. Bred with local sporting dogs, they served as the foundation for the Chesapeake Bay retriever breed.

HISTORY
AND
GOVERNMENT

SEAMAN

THE DOG WHO SAVED LEWIS AND CLARK

One of the most remarkable facts about the Lewis and Clark expedition is that just a single man was killed among the small group of explorers who traversed the untamed North American continent all the way to the Pacific coast and back. But without the quick thinking of a massive black Newfoundland named Seaman, the record could have been much worse.

Lewis, the cocaptain of the expedition, had purchased the dog in Pittsburgh for the then-princely sum of twenty dollars. The investment paid for itself on May 29, 1805, as the team bivouacked on the banks of the Missouri River in what is now central Montana. While the group slept, an enormous bull buffalo swam the river and charged into the camp, making a beeline for the tent where Clark and Lewis rested. At the last minute, Seaman appeared from nowhere, got between the enraged animal and the tent, and raised such a ruckus that the buffalo veered off into the night, never to be seen again. Twenty dollars may have been a lot of money for a dog in those days, but considering Seaman's contribution to the expedition, it was the best money Lewis ever spent.

LILINE

THE DOG WHO ALMOST SAVED THE KING OF FRANCE

King Henri III of France loved papillons. He kept a pack of the little dogs and spent lavishly to maintain them—he also attended council meetings with papillon-filled baskets suspended around his neck, angering his advisors. Perhaps they were upset because there was little time for such frivolity; Henri III lived in turbulent times, and he was almost constantly involved in religious wars between Catholics (whom he championed) and Protestants.

On the night of August 1, 1589, Henri encamped with his army in Saint Cloud on his way to lay siege to Paris. Before he retired, a monk named Jacques Clement, who had asked to see him, was admitted into his presence. Henri's favorite papillon, Liline, took an instant dislike to the man, barking so hysterically that she had to be taken from the room. Ignoring her reaction cost the king dearly.

The monk pulled out a knife and stabbed the king in the stomach. Poor Henri III lingered for several days before finally expiring. It was long enough to reflect on the folly of ignoring the warning of his best advisor—and surest judge of character—tiny Liline.

KEES

THE DOG WHO BECAME A POLITICAL SYMBOL

Holland's unofficial national dog is a fuzzy, medium-sized creature called the keeshond. Used for centuries to guard canal barges, the breed was nearly driven into extinction when it ended up on the losing side of a high-stakes political dispute—the same dispute, ironically, that gave the breed its name.

In the 1770s, populist forces battled the ruling House of Orange for control of the Low Countries. Their leader was Cornelis de Gyselaer, a man who was constantly shadowed by a furry gray dog known by his master's nickname, Kees. The canine, and the breed in general, became the movement's symbol—a fact that almost spelled doom for the dogs when the House of Orange regained power. Suddenly Kees and all his compatriots were very unfashionable. The poor keeshond (translation: Kees's hound) was saved from oblivion in the early twentieth century, when the Baroness van Hardenbroek rounded up surviving examples of the rebel dog and formed a viable breeding population. Today the keeshond is popular again throughout Holland—even though it isn't recognized there as a purebred.

FALA

PRESIDENT FRANKLIN D. ROOSEVELT'S CANINE MASCOT

Franklin D. Roosevelt was elected president of the United States for an unprecedented four terms, leading the nation through both the Great Depression and World War II. During his decade and a half in office, his most famous, most beloved associate (after his wife, Eleanor) was most likely Fala, a Scottish terrier who brightened the last five years of his life.

Fala came to the White House on November 10, 1940, the gift of one of Roosevelt's cousins. He was originally named Big Boy, until the president changed it to Murray the Outlaw of Falahill (a reference to a Scottish ancestor), then shortened that mouthful to "Fala." Shortly after his arrival at the executive mansion, the little dog had to go to the vet for treatment of severe stomach trouble. A quick investigation revealed the cause: Everyone on the White House staff, from presidential aides to kitchen personnel, was slipping him snacks. To avoid such problems in the future, Roosevelt decreed that the only food Fala would eat would come from him.

The little dog accompanied the president everywhere. Fala attended the Atlantic Charter Conference in Quebec and talks with the president of Mexico in Monterey. Fala was even sucked into a political dustup. During the 1944 presidential election campaign, Roosevelt's Republican opponents put out a story that, during a tour of the Aleutian Islands off the coast of Alaska, the president had diverted a navy destroyer to pick up Fala, who had been left behind at one of his stops.

This "scandal" was put to rest on September 23, 1944, when FDR gave what came to be known as his "Fala speech." During a Washington, D.C., campaign dinner, he enumerated the various bad things his opponents had said about him, saving the Fala incident for last. "These Republican leaders have not been content with attacks on me, or my wife, or on my sons," Roosevelt said. "No, not content with that, they now include my little dog, Fala. Well, of course, I don't resent attacks, and my family doesn't resent attacks—but Fala does resent them. You know, Fala is Scotch, and being a Scottie, as soon as he learned that the Republican fiction writers in Congress and out had concocted a story that I had left him behind on the Aleutian Islands and had sent a destroyer back to find him—at a cost to the taxpayers of two or three, or eight or twenty million dollars—his Scotch soul was furious. He has not been the same dog since!"

Fala was not forgotten even after Roosevelt's death in April 1945. The little dog rode the funeral train from Warm Springs, Georgia, to Washington, D.C., and was present for the burial service.

Afterward he lived with Eleanor Roosevelt and was often mentioned in her long-running syndicated newspaper column, *My Day*.

Yet throughout the remainder of his long life, Fala never forgot FDR. When the two had traveled together, their car was almost always escorted by police with sirens blaring. Even in old age, Fala's ears would perk up when he heard the sound of sirens, as if he believed Roosevelt might be coming home.

The two were finally reunited in 1952, when Fala passed away and was laid to rest beside Roosevelt in Hyde Park, New York. Today, at the Franklin Delano Roosevelt Memorial in Washington, D.C., a life-size statue of Fala sits dutifully beside a likeness of his master, just as in real life.

CHECKERS

THE DOG WHO SAVED RICHARD NIXON'S POLITICAL CAREER

More than twenty years before Watergate, Richard Nixon found himself embroiled in a political scandal so damaging that he had to call upon his dog, Checkers, to save his career.

As the vice-presidential running mate of Dwight D. Eisenhower in 1952, Nixon was accused of accepting some $18,000 in illegal campaign contributions. The charge severely injured his reputation, so much so that Eisenhower seemed ready to drop him from the ticket. Something extraordinary had to be done.

On September 23, 1952, Nixon offered a nationally televised response that came to be called the "Checkers speech." He revealed his rather modest finances, giving the impression of being a middle-class "man of the people" in the process. But what really won over Joe Public was his reference to Checkers, a cocker spaniel given to his family by a well-wisher. "The kids, like all kids, love the dog and I just want to say this right now, that regardless of what they say about it, we're gonna keep it."

The speech preserved Nixon's career—at least for a while. And it won Checkers a place in political history.

BECERRILLO

THE SPANISH WAR DOG WHO SHAMED THE CONQUISTADORS

The story of the Spanish conquest of Central and South America is written in blood—most of it Native American. Nations large and small fell to the conquistadors, who again and again crushed numerically superior forces using European "wonder weapons" such as firearms and cavalry.

One of the greatest of these wonder weapons was the war dog—huge canines who were incredibly strong, seemingly immune to physical pain, and trained to fight alongside their masters in battle. They proved devastating against lightly armed and armored Native American warriors. The conquistadors, knowing that the locals were terrified of these enormous, bloodthirsty killers, took them with them wherever they went. They were as useful for intimidation as they were for battle.

One of the most famous was named Becerrillo ("the little bull"). During Becerrillo's time in the New World, his bloody reputation loomed so large that enemies would flee the field at the very sight of him. "He attacked his foes with fury and rage and defended his friends with great valor," says the famous account, *A Brief Chronicle of the Destruction of the Indies*. "The Indians were more afraid of ten Spanish soldiers accompanied by

Becerrillo than by 100 soldiers without him."

After fighting in numerous engagements, Becerrillo's body was covered with battle scars. In exchange for his service, he was treated like a regular soldier and even got a cut of the booty—though what use a dog might have for such possessions is hard to imagine.

Although the huge fighting dog gained a well-deserved reputation for ferocity in battle, there were some actions to which he wouldn't stoop. The story is told of how, after a rout of Native American fighters on the island of Puerto Rico, Becerrillo's handler, Diego de Salazar, thought up a "game" for the entertainment of his comrades. In the aftermath of the battle, Salazar and his friends had nothing to do but await the arrival of the territorial governor—the legendary Juan Ponce de León. Salazar called over an old Native American woman, gave her a piece of paper, told her it contained a message for the governor, and ordered her to take it to him immediately, on pain of death. The terrified woman started walking. A few moments later, Salazar commanded Becerrillo to attack her.

According to tales from the time, the great dog launched himself at his target with fangs bared, and the old woman fell to her knees and begged her would-be killer for mercy. Then something strange happened. Incredibly, Becerrillo, who is reckoned to have slaughtered scores of human beings in battle, defied his master's instructions. He sniffed curiously at the woman, then turned around and walked away.

His conquistador friends were aghast, to say the least. Some were so shaken by the dog's actions that they claimed it must have been caused by divine intervention. Others were ashamed that a dog refused to commit the sort of cold-blooded murder that his human compatriots would have done without a second thought.

Not long afterward, Ponce de León arrived and was told the story. He ordered the old woman to be freed and returned to her people, then commanded that no further acts of vengeance be carried out against the local population. "I will not permit the compassion and forgiveness of a dog to outshine that of a true Christian," he reportedly said.

Becerrillo was, indeed, a killer. But unlike his friends, he wasn't a murderer.

SAUR

THE DOG WHO BECAME A NORWEGIAN KING

Ancient Viking chronicles tell a strange tale of twelfth-century political intrigue. There are various versions of the story, but the most common goes like this: When Norwegian king Eystein Magnusson conquered the land of Throndhjem, he appointed his son, Onund, to rule in his stead. But the people killed Onund and rose in rebellion. Magnusson, who was more than a little angry about the revolt and the loss of his child, crushed all resistance with great ferocity.

After the fighting stopped, the irate king offered the survivors a choice of leadership. They could either bow and swear eternal loyalty to his slave—a man named Thorer Faxe—or they could take as their leader the sovereign's dog, Saur (an obscenity that means "excrement").

The people reportedly accepted the dog, on the notion that because dogs don't live all that long, they would be free of him sooner. History doesn't say how long they had to endure this humiliation. But it does state that Saur was given a throne, a court, a lavish home, and even a collar of gold.

BICHE

THE DOG WHO ALMOST DESTROYED THE KINGDOM OF PRUSSIA

For centuries, the country we now call Germany was nothing but a loose collection of tiny kingdoms, municipalities, and city-states. Not surprisingly, they were easy prey for the larger European nations surrounding them. It wasn't until the sixteenth century that the Kingdom of Prussia, a miniscule bit of territory on the periphery of Central Europe, began a long rise to prominence that would culminate in its forging a united German Empire in the late nineteenth century.

Prussia didn't begin life as a great power, however. The kingdom had to survive for centuries as a relatively powerless flyspeck caught between not-always-friendly giants, including France, Russia, and Austria. Fortunately, it was ably led. One of Prussia's greatest rulers was King Frederick II—better known as Frederick the Great. He was an astute politician and military leader who did everything from reform his nation's school system to increase Prussia's influence through victorious wars of expansion during his forty-six-year reign. But Frederick wasn't infallible—one coarse, dog-related pun nearly cost him his throne.

The sovereign spent most of his life walking a political tightrope. Shortly after ascending to the kingship in 1740, he wrested some territory from the Austrian Empire in a short, bitter conflict. Austria's ruler, Empress Maria Theresa, never forgot the humiliation. For years she plotted her revenge, building up her own army, arranging a military alliance with Russia, and desperately trying to reach a similar understanding with France.

Frederick's love of dogs—and his own loose lips—would help the empress close the deal. The Prussian king had few friends and displayed no interest in women. His strongest emotional bond was with his pack of Italian greyhounds. The little creatures followed him everywhere and even shared his bed. His personal favorite was a female named Biche, who was allowed to sit on his lap during state meetings.

Unfortunately, Frederick had a sarcastic streak that he sometimes applied to people who didn't take kindly to kidding. One evening during a reception at his palace, the conversation turned to King Louis XV of France and his mistress, Madame de Pompadour. She had started out merely as the king's paramour, but her astute political instincts transformed her into one of Louis's most influential advisors. But that evening Frederick offered a far-less-flattering estimation to his dining companions—gesturing toward Biche, who sat near him, he said that the dog was *his* Madame de

Pompadour. The only difference was that instead of bestowing her the title of Marquise, he'd given his "advisor" the title of Biche. Which, of course, translates to "bitch" in English.

Not surprisingly, word of this incident quickly got back to Pompadour. Incensed, she convinced the French king to join the anti-Prussian alliance. In a little dustup that would come to be called the Seven Years' War, Austria, France, Russia, and several smaller powers united to wipe Prussia off the map. Only Frederick's brilliant generalship—and the timely death of the Russian Czarina, who despised him almost as much as Maria Theresa—saved his kingdom from annihilation.

During the desperate conflict Biche served alongside the king. She followed his horse into battle, narrowly escaping death on several occasions. Once she was even captured by Hungarian troops but was repatriated to the overjoyed Frederick after lengthy negotiations. Apparently, though Madame de Pompadour never forgave Frederick for comparing her to a dog, the dog didn't mind being compared to a French mistress.

DEMPSEY

THE DOG WHO ESCAPED A DEATH SENTENCE

England doesn't have a death penalty for humans, but it does have one for dogs. During the 1990s, an American pit pull terrier named Dempsey was almost its first victim. Instead, she became the center of an international firestorm over animal rights.

England's Dangerous Dogs Act of 1991 was passed after several highly publicized canine attacks on children. The act made it illegal to own "dangerous" breeds (specifically, the Fila Brasileiro, Dogo Argentino, Tosa, and pit bull terriers) without a court exemption and required those who were exempt to be keep their dogs leashed and muzzled at all times in public. The penalty for failing to comply was death—not for the irresponsible owner, but for the dog.

That's where matters stood when Dempsey, a six-year-old female American pit bull owned by London resident Dianne Fanneran, was taken for a walk by one of Fanneran's friends on an April evening in 1992. Dempsey started the trip properly leashed and muzzled, but when she began choking, her human companion removed the muzzle so she could vomit. The infraction was spotted by two passing police officers, who swooped in and "arrested" Dempsey. Three months later, at Ealing Magistrates' Court, she was sentenced to death under the Dangerous Dogs Act.

Thus began a three-year-long legal ordeal for Fanneran and her luckless dog, who spent the time cooling her heels in various municipal kennels. The case trudged through the British legal system, eventually getting bumped up all the way to the House of Lords—and then back down to the lower courts. In the meantime animal-rights advocates rallied to Dempsey's side, loudly protesting the unfairness of this case in particular and the law in general. Actress and animal rights activist Brigitte Bardot even offered the put-upon pit bull political asylum in France.

Finally, in November 2002, the case was dismissed—not because government officials had seen the folly of their ways, but because of a technicality. Fanneran, it seems, hadn't been informed of her dog's first court date in advance, as the law required. Dempsey went free and lived to the ripe old age of seventeen. But the much-maligned Dangerous Dogs Act remains on the books. In 2002 it even snagged Princess Anne, the daughter of Queen Elizabeth II, when one of her bull terriers attacked two children. Her dog didn't get the death penalty, but Princess Anne was fined £500.

OWNEY

THE MASCOT OF THE UNITED STATES POSTAL SERVICE

Most dogs seem to instinctively despise postal employees. But one canine developed a decidedly more charitable view of them—perhaps because he owed his life, his livelihood, and his considerable fame to the kindness of these civil servants.

The poor dog was abandoned as a puppy in 1888 outside an Albany, New York, post office. The employees took pity on him and allowed him to stay the night, curled up on a pile of empty mailbags. Owney, as he came to be called, never seemed to forget that first act of kindness. He adored the smell of mailbags his entire life and would follow just about anyone who carried one. He started shadowing letter carriers, then hitched rides on Albany-area mail wagons, then started hopping the Railway Post Office (RPO) train cars that crisscrossed New York state. Soon he was traveling the entire country by rail, always under the watchful care of the RPO clerks.

Whenever Owney visited a new locale, the area's postal workers marked the occasion by affixing medals or tags to his collar. Eventually these became so numerous, and so heavy, that the postmaster general, John Wanamaker, had a special harness created so Owney would have more places on which to display them. Even then, most of the hundreds he accumulated simply had to be stored away. If he'd worn them all, Owney wouldn't have been able to move.

His greatest excursion came in 1895, when the postmaster of Tacoma, Washington, sent Owney on a world tour. The dog and his own personal postal clerk visited Asia and the Middle East and traversed the continental United States before returning to Tacoma after 113 days on the road.

During his lifetime, it's estimated that Owney traveled some 140,000 miles (225,000 km) in the company of various letter carriers. When he passed away in 1897, despondent mail clerks raised money to have him stuffed. After years in a glass case at the Post Office Department's Washington, D.C., headquarters, he was transferred to the Smithsonian Institution in 1911. Today he resides in the National Postal Museum, still wearing his original, medal-covered harness.

POMPEY

THE DOG WHO SAVED A DYNASTY

The man known as the father of the Netherlands, William I, Prince of Orange, rose to power after years of political maneuvering and bitter warfare. But save for the vigilance of a lowly pug named Pompey, the man who led the Dutch to freedom might have died at the end of a Spanish sword.

William, a native German, became governor of the Low Countries in 1559 at the behest of Philip II, King of Spain. But the Spanish ruled the area with such an iron hand that William and the native Dutch grew restive. Finally, the population rose in rebellion, and William helped to lead the way. The Spanish were finally expelled after years of bloody war, and seventeen tiny Low Country states were welded into the nation known as the Netherlands. William, now called the "Father of the fatherland," was made hereditary ruler, and the Dutch flag and coat of arms were based on his own livery and arms. Most importantly, his direct descendant, William III of Orange, would become King of England and Scotland.

But all that glory would have seemed like a fantasy in 1572, when William was still in the thick of the war with Spain. One evening, after his army had encamped and he'd gone to bed, the Spanish launched a daring midnight attack. The assault took the Dutch by complete surprise. But as the prince slept next to his beloved pet pug Pompey, the little dog heard the Spanish and roused his master with his barking. William, who might have been killed or captured in the unanticipated attack, bolted from his tent and rode away, barely escaping capture or death.

From that day forward, in honor of Pompey's actions, William always kept a pug at his side—a pug was even carved on his tomb. And for as long as the dynasty lasted, the little dogs who saved the House of Orange were strongly associated with its members.

THE FISHERMAN'S NEWFOUNDLAND

THE DOG WHO HELPED NAPOLEON MEET HIS WATERLOO

Napoleon Bonaparte, Emperor of France, is said to have loathed dogs, so he must have found it particularly galling to owe his life to one.

In 1814 a coalition that included Great Britain, Russia, and Prussia banished Napoleon to the island of Elba, a spot of land just off the Italian coast. But after only ten months on this island prison, Napoleon arranged to escape and return to France. To foil British naval patrols, he plotted to leave in a small boat, under cover of darkness, on a rainy, stormy night; a particularly dangerous plot for a landlubber like Napoleon who, by some accounts, couldn't even swim.

At the appointed hour he gamely boarded an open boat, which was to row him through the rough water to the French warship *Inconstant*. At some point, perhaps to appear more heroic, the great conqueror made the extremely unwise decision to stand up in the tiny vessel's pitching gunwale—a nearly fatal error. Napoleon fell overboard into the dark Mediterranean. The boat's crew, straining at their oars, failed to notice his disappearance and kept rowing, leaving him behind.

The only creature who noted his unscheduled departure was a black-and-white Newfoundland dog aboard a nearby fishing vessel. The dog leapt into the water and swam to the struggling man, who clung to him for dear life during the precious minutes it took for the men on the boat to realize they needed to turn around. Napoleon was eventually hauled back aboard, cold and exhausted but alive, thanks to the timely intervention of a fisherman's companion.

The dog, no doubt, returned to his master's vessel, never to know the pivotal role he'd just played in history. Napoleon toweled off, returned to France, and seized the reins of power. His numerous enemies rallied against him, and the two forces met on June 18, 1815, at the fateful battle that forever ended the emperor's dreams of power—Waterloo.

After great loss of life, Napoleon's plan to conquer Europe ended. Few now realize that, save for the heroism of a lowly Elban dog, his last bid to rule the continent never would have happened.

BOYE

THE DOG WHO NEVER LOST A BATTLE

During the English Civil War, one of the most able men in the service of the king was Prince Rupert of the Rhine. King Charles appointed Rupert, a born warrior and expert horseman, to lead the Royalist cavalry in 1642. The bold and audacious Rupert won numerous battles against Charles's enemies.

Some ascribed his success to brilliant tactics, but others saw something more sinister. According to history, Rupert's constant companion was a white standard poodle named Boye. The prince's enemies believed that the dog was a demon who assisted him with magic. Drawings of Rupert from that time routinely show him in the company of the dog. Interestingly, pictures rendered by his opponents portray Boye not as a poodle, but as some sort of macabre wolf-dragon hybrid.

Perhaps Rupert's adversaries were on to something. The general and Boye advanced from victory to victory until the fateful battle of Marston Moor. There, the poor dog was shot and killed by enemy soldiers, and Rupert, for almost the first time in his military career, went down in defeat.

FORTUNE

THE DOG WHO KEPT THE BONAPARTES APART

Sometimes, very small dogs can play very large roles in human history. Consider the life of Fortune, a pug who belonged to a French noblewoman named Marie-Josephe-Rose de Beauharnais. Rose, as she was known, was imprisoned after the French Revolution simply because she was an aristocrat, as was her husband, Vicomte Alexandre Beauharnais.

But worse was to come. Alexandre Beauharnais was guillotined, and it looked like his wife would soon follow him unless she was able to do something to save her life. Rose was forbidden to send letters to those in the outside world, and she was allowed to receive only a handful of closely scrutinized human visitors. However, she was permitted routine visits with her pug, Fortune. Her jailors never realized that most days the little dog left her company with a note from Rose tucked under her velvet collar, addressed to her influential friends who remained in power. When a change in the French government removed the threat of imminent execution, her associates were able to secure her release.

It's no wonder, then, that Rose prized her tiny coconspirator so highly. The little dog slept with her, and nothing, not even the presence of a new husband, could change that—even though the new husband happened to be Napoleon Bonaparte, soon-to-be emperor of France. Napoleon, whom she met shortly after her release from jail, preferred to call his bride Josephine rather than Rose. The two were married on March 9, 1796; but there was a slight problem on their wedding night. Fortune, accustomed to sleeping alone with Josephine, wasn't inclined to give up her spot to a usurper. Nevertheless, Napoleon, uninterested in having an audience on his honeymoon, wanted her removed. Josephine, according to legend, told the emperor, "If the pug doesn't sleep in our bed, neither do I!"

Napoleon, undeterred, attempted to scoop up Fortune in his arms. And for his troubles, he received a savage bite, the scar from which he would carry for the rest of his life. Thus the great conqueror went down in defeat in the bedroom.

GENERAL HOWE'S DOG

THE DOG WHO SWITCHED SIDES DURING THE AMERICAN REVOLUTION

One of the most curious dog-related incidents that took place during the American Revolution occurred on October 4, 1777, at the Battle of Germantown. Fought just outside of Philadelphia, it pitted the British army, commanded by General William Howe, against the Continental Army, under the command of General George Washington. The bloody all-day struggle finally ended when the Americans, outmaneuvered and running low on supplies, were forced to disengage.

In the confusion that followed, one of the battle's participants took the opportunity to switch sides. Howe's dog followed his master onto the battlefield, but after the melee, the confused canine—who was no doubt much less interested in the political ramifications of the conflict than his human associates—retired from the field with the wrong army. Sometime later he was picked up by an American patrol, which quickly noted that his collar was inscribed with a silver tag stating that he belonged to the British commander. The animal was taken straight to Washington, and the entire matter (along with the dog) placed in his hands.

Some thought was probably given to keeping the canine as war booty. Instead, Washington, a dedicated dog lover, did something utterly unwarlike. After seeing that the animal was fed and cared for, he ordered it returned to the British lines with the following note: "General Washington's compliments to General Howe. He does himself the pleasure to return him a dog, which accidentally fell into his hands, and by the inscription on the Collar appear to belong to General Howe."

Reportedly, Howe was overjoyed at the unexpected return of his pet. And some say that he also found a second message from Washington secreted under the dog's collar on a tightly folded piece of paper. Its contents, if the story is true, are lost to history. But what is known is that Howe, who began his work in the Colonies intent on pursuing the rebellion to utter destruction, from that day forward seemed far less inclined to serve as the architect of the revolution's demise. Perhaps the simple act of returning the general's dog helped him see his enemies as humans, rather than merely as rebels.

URIAN

THE DOG WHO FOUNDED THE CHURCH OF ENGLAND

Everyone knows that England's Henry VIII had plenty of wives, but some might not realize that he went through so many paramours because he was desperate to find a woman who could give him a male heir. In 1525, angered at the inability of his first wife, Catherine of Aragon, to produce a son, he started dallying with a young courtier named Anne Boleyn. Soon he talked openly of divorcing Catherine and marrying his new love (or more likely, lust) interest.

Trouble was, he'd need to have the marriage annulled by the pope. But the Catholic Church refused to grant his request, especially since Henry had received a special dispensation to enable him to marry Catherine in the first place. Nevertheless, Henry spent years and a great deal of money trying to get Pope Clement VII to see things his way. Finally, after endless negotiations by Cardinal Wolsey, the king's deputy, Henry seemed on the verge of getting what he wanted. Legend says Wolsey was to meet with Clement personally to hammer out the last details.

According to the story, Wolsey brought his favorite greyhound, Urian, with him on his visit to the pope. Like a proper gentleman, he tied the dog discreetly at the door and approached the pope with the intent of kissing the pontiff's foot.

Unfortunately, Urian didn't understand what was going on. When he saw the pope raise his foot, the dog jumped to the conclusion that the pontiff planned to attack his master. Urian struck first, streaking into the room and savagely biting the pope's ankle. Clement, bleeding and in pain, hobbled away as fast as his wounded appendage would carry him, all the while vowing never to make a deal with Henry VIII.

Wolsey was disgraced, and Henry, still intent on producing an heir, was forced to take drastic measures. In 1533 he married Anne Boleyn, cut

ties with the Catholic Church, and, shortly thereafter, declared himself head of the new Church of England. One wonders if, once faced with the ramifications of his anger, the pope ever wished he'd simply wrapped a bandage around his foot and continued with his meeting.

SHANDA

THE DOG WHO WAS MAYOR OF A TOWN

For a long time the little principality of Guffey, Colorado, was more ghost town than town. Located on the southern end of a large mountain valley called South Park (the one after which the animated television series is named), Guffey reached its high point at the end of the nineteenth century, when gold prospectors turned it into a classic frontier boomtown. Unfortunately there wasn't enough ore in the ground to sustain the town's growth, and the community was just about deserted only a few years after its heyday.

Today the town is known for three things—its Old West–style architecture, which the handful of locals endeavor mightily to preserve; an annual Chicken Fly festival, in which live chickens are tossed off a fifteen-foot-tall (4.6 m) tower to see how far their stubby wings can carry them; and the fact that during the 1990s the community's "mayor" was a golden retriever named Shanda.

The dog's rise to power began in 1988, when Park County officials in the nearby community of Fairplay realized they had lost the town plat for Guffey. A new map was created, placing the town's roughly two dozen residents in a commercial zone rather than a residential one and radically increasing their taxes. The locals then mounted a rebellion of sorts, establishing their own "existing transitional" zone with a more lenient tax structure. For good measure, they also elected a series of cats as mayor—first a feline named Paisley, then another named Smudge le Plume, and finally a calico named Whifley le Gone. When Whifley left office in 1993 to live on a ranch, the position was usurped by Shanda.

In a coup d'état of sorts, she got the job because her master, Bruce Buffington, purchased the town general store, which also contained the mayor's office. Not surprisingly, putting a dog in charge caught the attention of the media. Buffington and Shanda appeared together on *The Oprah Winfrey Show*. But the dog's reign only lasted through 1998, when the residents of Guffey elected another cat, Monster, to the job. His office is a ratty couch in front of an old garage that houses a store called Last Chance Antiques.

SAUCISSE

THE DOG WHO RAN FOR PRESIDENT OF FRANCE

The French presidential election of 2002 proved a decidedly uninteresting, uninspiring affair. The two top candidates were incumbent Jacques Chirac, who was hamstrung by multiple political scandals. His chief rival was the widely disliked, archconservative (at least by French standards) Socialist prime minister Lionel Jospin. Chirac won handily, with 82 percent of the vote. The electorate was so underwhelmed by the choice of contenders that some of Chirac's own supporters backed him with the tepid rallying cry, "Vote for the crook, not the fascist."

The only other options were supplied by a handful of smaller parties and individuals, none of whom had any real chance of winning, but several of whom were anything but boring. Take, for instance, the candidacy of a dog named Saucisse. This politically minded canine was an electoral veteran, having won 4 percent of the vote in a municipal election in Marseille.

On the strength of this modest performance, Saucisse joined the large pool of small-fry candidates seeking the presidency. At first glance the tiny former stray seemed perfect for the dog-eat-dog world of politics, having already survived the even more dog-eat-dog world of dog fighting, where the smallish canine (whose name translates to "sausage" in English) was used as bait to motivate the combatants. Alas, his drive for the executive office was short-lived. He was weeded out before the general election for failing to obtain signatures from a minimum of five hundred of France's *grands electeurs*—a group of roughly fifty thousand mid-level politicians, including mayors, deputies, and representatives from the country's overseas territories. The signatures are required to keep "frivolous" candidates out, but opponents call it an undemocratic roadblock to wider electoral participation.

It's too bad five hundred couldn't be talked into supporting Saucisse. Even if his presence on the ballot would have been somewhat frivolous, it would have been interesting. Boredom—and public disillusionment with politicians of the two-legged variety—is what gave Saucisse his (admittedly small) popular appeal. "Saucisse is sending a warning to politicians that unless they do better we would rather vote for a dog," said the canine's owner, Serge Scotto.

OTHER CANINES OF DISTINCTION

LADDIE BOY: U.S. president Warren G. Harding's pet Airedale. Some 19,000 newspaper boys each chipped in a penny to create a copper statue of him.

WILLY: The bull terrier who served as the wartime companion of U.S. general George S. Patton. Named William the Conqueror, he became "Willy" because of his timid nature.

NERO: The original watchdog of the United States Mint in Philadelphia. According to legend, the old version of the Treasury's seal showed Nero guarding the key to a mint strongbox.

BELFERLEIN: A Pomeranian owned by Protestant Reformation leader Martin Luther and who is mentioned many times in his printed works. To reassure his children that their pets would have someplace to go after they died, Luther went out of his way to state that dogs are allowed in heaven.

MARIE ANTOINETTE'S PAPILLION: This tiny toy canine accompanied the queen of France to the guillotine. After her execution, the dog was adopted by a family who lived in a Paris domicile now known as Papillion House.

ARTS
AND
LITERATURE

GELERT

THE LOYAL DOG WHO INSPIRED A LEGEND

Near the North Wales town of Beddgelert lies a tree-shaded, grass-covered mound that supposedly houses the remains of a noble hunting dog—a dog even more noble than his owner, a prince of Wales. Their tragic misunderstanding provides the grist for one of Wales's saddest legends.

The story is commonly believed to have unfolded in the twelfth century, when King John of England gave a mighty hunting dog named Gelert to his Welsh ally, Llewelyn the Great. The dog and the king became fast friends, and Gelert was soon so trusted that he was tasked with the important job of guarding Llewelyn's infant son. But then one day tragedy struck—the king found the baby's bed-chamber overturned, his cradle empty, and Gelert standing nearby with blood on his muzzle. Assuming the worst, the king drew his sword and slew the dog. Only then did he hear the cries of his son. He found him under his cradle, unharmed—with a dead wolf nearby. Gelert had saved him. Llewelyn, overcome with remorse, gave the hound a hero's funeral in the town of Beddgelert (which means "grave of Gelert" in Welsh). It stands as a memorial to canine faithfulness and to the dangers of jumping to conclusions.

BLAIR

THE FIRST CANINE MOVIE STAR

Ask almost anyone to name the first collie to make it big in films, and chances are they won't say "Blair." Yet in 1905, decades before Lassie's big-screen debut, an innocuous family dog by that name became a sensation in the British film *Rescued by Rover*.

The six-minute silent flick was the brainchild of producer Cecil M. Hepworth. Considered one of the lowest-budget films ever made, it featured the story of a dog who saves a baby who's been kidnapped by gypsies.

Rescued by Rover was very much a family affair. Hepworth's wife came up with the story; she and Hepworth (who also codirected, produced, and helped build the sets) played the stolen baby's parents; their infant daughter, Elizabeth, served as the baby; and the title role of Rover was tackled by the family pet, a diminutive collie named Blair. The entire project was scripted, filmed, and edited in a matter of days, for a reported seven pounds, thirteen shillings, and sixpence.

The movie was an instant sensation. *Rescued by Rover* became so popular that Hepworth had to reshoot it two more times, because the original film was worn out from making endless prints. In all, some four hundred copies were distributed worldwide.

Not surprisingly, the project inspired a couple of sequels. In the first, *Dumb Sagacity* (1907), "Rover" was paired with a horse who had starred a year earlier in Hepworth's shoestring production of *Black Beauty*. A 1908 film with the not-very-imaginative title *The Dog Outwits the Kidnappers* stuck more closely to the first story that made Rover famous. In it, the Hepworth family pet rescued yet another baby by spiriting it away, this time in an automobile. This "special effect" was accomplished by having Blair sit on the driver's seat with her front paws propped on the steering wheel. Hepworth, crouching out of sight on the floorboards, did the actual driving.

Today *Rescued by Rover* is remembered for two major reasons. For one thing, it pioneered some

fairly sophisticated editing techniques that would soon become standard tools in all films. For another, it made Blair's onscreen moniker a household word. Before the movie, almost no one called their dogs Rover. After it, so many people used the name, it became a cliché.

BEAUTIFUL JOE

THE MISTREATED DOG WHOSE "LIFE" BECAME A BESTSELLING NOVEL

Many authors suffer to gain literary fame, but few suffered as much as a poor nineteenth-century Canadian mongrel named Beautiful Joe. The dog lived in the town of Meaford, Ontario, and spent his early years in the clutches of a brutal, physically abusive owner who cut off his ears and tail. He was rescued in 1890 by a local woman, Louise Moore, who nursed him back to health—and, in spite of his appearance, named him Beautiful Joe. Not long afterward, Moore's fiancé's sister, writer Margaret Marshall Saunders, came to the little town for an extended visit. She was so moved by Beautiful Joe's heartrending story of survival that she decided to write a novel about him.

Actually, she decided to ghost author a book under his name. Using the peculiar device of writing as if her four-legged friend were telling the story—an approach pioneered with considerable success in the then-recently released *Black Beauty*—she penned an "autobiography" of the luckless canine called simply *Beautiful Joe*. Published in 1894, the book became an immediate sensation. It was the first Canadian book to sell more than a million copies (sales surpassed seven million by the late 1930s) and was translated into more than a dozen languages. A sequel, *Beautiful Joe's Paradise*, was published in 1902.

In 1934 Saunders was made a Commander of the British Empire in recognition of her help in advancing animal welfare. The book's first-person tone served to "humanize" the suffering of its animal protagonist in a way a more conventionally written account might never have done.

The story had a happy ending, both in literature and real life. After he escaped his brutal owner, Beautiful Joe lived a long and interesting life. He even got the satisfaction of bringing his former owner to justice by catching him in the act of breaking into a house. Today the town commemorates him with Beautiful Joe Park, located in the heart of Meaford, not too far from where Joe spent his happiest days.

MAN RAY

THE DOG WHO BECAME A WORK OF ART

Few great artists enjoyed the attention of a muse as constant and obedient—not to mention as hairy—as the one who helped make the career of William Wegman. The photographer is world famous for taking pictures of his pets—an entire platoon of dour, reserved-looking Weimaraners. His photos hang in cultural institutions around the world, including the Whitney Museum of American Art and the Smithsonian American Art Museum.

Wegman's foray into dog photography was accidental. Originally trained as a painter, he was teaching at California State University, Long Beach, when he acquired a hulking Weimaraner he named Man Ray, after the expressionist artist of the same name. At the time, Wegman was trying to shoot conceptual videos, and Man Ray kept barging into the scenes. Instead of shooing him away, the artist decided to let nature take its course and filmed the dog. Man Ray, with his deadpan expressions, turned out to be a natural. By the mid '70s Wegman's photos and videos gained both critical acclaim and a huge popular audience, appearing everywhere from exclusive gallery shows to *Saturday Night Live* and *The Tonight Show*.

Not surprisingly, the artist felt a bit nonplussed

that people only seemed interested in looking at snapshots of his pet. For a year he stopped taking Man Ray's picture. But in 1978, his faithful collaborator developed a severe case of prostate cancer—so severe that Wegman's vet recommended euthanasia. Instead, Wegman opted for aggressive treatment, and Man Ray survived. His master swore off his no-photos vow, and soon the Weimaraner was everywhere again. By the time of Man Ray's passing in 1982, he was such a fixture in the New York City art scene that the *Village Voice* dubbed him "Man of the Year."

His work was carried on several years later, when Wegman acquired (and began to photograph) a female Weimaraner named Fay Ray. And when Fay had a litter of ten puppies in 1989, a franchise was born. Today Wegman's pack appears on everything from postcards to refrigerator magnets.

BOATSWAIN

THE DOG WHOSE DEATH INSPIRED A CLASSIC POEM

The nineteenth-century poet Lord George Gordon Byron was, by all accounts, quite a piece of work. A leading figure in the Romantic movement, he was a prolific writer who produced verse of undeniable genius. He even helped inspire his friend, Mary Wollstonecraft Shelley, to write *Frankenstein* during an impromptu ghost story contest.

But while his poems were sublime, his private and public existence were often ridiculous. Described by one of his many, many ex-lovers as "mad, bad, and dangerous to know," he spent most of his short life living extravagantly, running up huge debts, enjoying erotic interludes with everyone from noblewomen to scullery maids, and participating, sometimes at great personal risk, in various European revolutionary movements. It was during one of these improbable adventures—fighting for Greek independence from the Ottoman Empire in 1824—that he died of fever.

Among his many near-obsessive interests, Byron was a legendary lover of animals. He owned, at various times in his life, a badger, an eagle, a crocodile, a bear, and numerous other creatures. But no member of his vast menagerie was closer to his heart than a Newfoundland named Boatswain.

For a time, the two were inseparable companions. When the dog contracted rabies, Byron cared for him personally, disregarding the very real danger of being bitten. And when the animal died and was laid to rest, Byron authored one of his best-known works in honor of his friend. Called *Epitaph to a Dog*, its loving words could be applied to almost any faithful canine who has ever brightened a human life with his or her presence. It reads in part:

Near this Spot
are deposited the Remains of one
who possessed Beauty without Vanity,
Strength without Insolence,
Courage without Ferosity,
and all the Virtues of Man without his Vices.
This praise, which would be unmeaning Flattery
if inscribed over human Ashes,
is but a just tribute to the Memory of
BOATSWAIN, a DOG,
who was born in Newfoundland May 1803,
and died at Newstead Nov. 18, 1808

Byron's companion lies in Newstead Abbey in a grave marked with a monument that bears the poet's tribute—and which is larger than the monument over the grave of the poet himself.

BOUNCE

THE DOG WHO SAVED THE LIFE OF ALEXANDER POPE

Alexander Pope was one of the premier poets of the early eighteenth century. Though the casual reader might not know his larger works, such as *The Rape of the Lock*, almost everyone remembers his pithy witticisms and observations. It was Pope who invented such time-honored phrases as, "To err is human, to forgive, divine," and "For fools rush in where angels fear to tread." But many of those remarks might never have been uttered without the timely intervention of Pope's Great Dane, Bounce.

Throughout his life, Pope always kept large dogs—usually Great Danes, usually named Bounce. They were part companions, part bodyguards. The poet's habit of attacking critics, other writers, and prominent professionals in his satirical works earned him a long list of ill-wishers, some of whom (Pope feared) might stoop to physical violence. And since Pope was only four feet, six inches (137 cm) tall and severely debilitated by a form of tuberculosis that attacks the spine, he wasn't a physical match for anyone. For this reason, according to his sister, he never went for walks without pistols in his pockets and his loyal dog Bounce at his side.

His vigilant canine companion did save his life one night, though not from someone he'd savaged in print. Pope's valet resigned unexpectedly and a replacement was quickly hunted down. But that very evening, Pope awoke in the middle of the night to find the new valet creeping up on his bed with a knife. Knowing the poet was too weak to resist, the man intended to kill him and steal the money Pope kept lying around the house. But the new valet hadn't anticipated the presence of Bounce, who sprang from beneath the bed, knocked the would-be killer to the floor, and summoned help with his thunderous barking.

With Bounce's help, Pope lived to write another day, and to make the following too-true observation: "Histories are more full of the examples of the fidelity of dogs than of friends."

PEPS AND FIPS

THE DOGS WHO HELPED WAGNER COMPOSE HIS OPERAS

The great composer Richard Wagner enjoyed a lifelong love affair with dogs, two of whom actually helped him work. The first, Peps, was a furry muse. Wagner would pound out notes on his piano, then glance over to see if Peps, who sat on his own stool, approved. Wagner noticed that the dog showed distinct reactions to certain musical phrases, giving him the then-new idea of associating particular melodies in his operas with specific characters, settings, or moods.

Armed with this dog-given insight, Wagner began the composition of his masterwork, a collection of four operas known collectively as *The Ring of the Nibelung*. But before the great maestro finished, Peps sickened and died. Wagner was devastated, but he soon acquired a new dog named Fips. One day, as he continued his work on the Ring cycle, Wagner took Fips for a walk in the park. As the dog darted back and forth, rustling through the dry leaves, the composer discerned a catchy

rhythm in Fips's steps, which he decided to incorporate into his music. Thus, in the opera *Siegfried*, the passage denoting the title character's journey through a forest is derived from the footfalls of Fips.

CHARLEY

THE DOG WHO INSPIRED JOHN STEINBECK

Plenty of novelists take on collaborators. Such was the case for John Steinbeck, the Pulitzer Prize–winning author of *East of Eden*, *Grapes of Wrath*, and many other important books. It was 1960, and Steinbeck, in his late fifties, was recovering from a stroke. But he didn't want to start acting like an invalid. Instead, he went on a road trip. He bought a customized motor home, which he named *Rocinante*, after Don Quixote's horse, and he and his traveling companion—his black standard poodle, Charley—hit the road on September 23, 1960. The two of them rambled for twelve thousand miles (19,000 km), through thirty-seven states plus parts of Canada, before returning to their New York home in January 1961.

As it turned out, Charley more than pulled his weight on the trip. The big poodle was a tremendously helpful icebreaker when Steinbeck sought to strike up conversations with strangers. If he wanted to chat, all he had to do was walk up to someone with Charley in tow. The dog was also a sympathetic listener; during the long drive the two apparently covered a lot of ground, discussing everything from the foibles of small-town life to racial discrimination. This more than made up for the fact that Charley's violent reaction to a bear he saw in the road forced their quick departure from Yellowstone National Park.

Steinbeck's account of the trip, appropriately called *Travels with Charley*, was published in the summer of 1961 to great popular and critical acclaim. Steinbeck passed away in 1968, but his chronicle of life on the road with his dog lives on. The trailer he used on his journey is preserved for posterity at the National Steinbeck Center in Salinas, California. And his traveling companion, the faithful Charley, is likewise preserved in Steinbeck's prose. "He is a good friend and traveling companion, and would rather travel about than anything he can imagine," he wrote. "If he occurs at length in this account, it is because he contributed much to the trip."

BLACK SHUCK

THE DEMON DOG WHO INSPIRED A FAMOUS NOVEL

For as long as humans have inhabited the swath of English coastline now known as East Anglia, tales have circulated concerning a gigantic black dog that haunts the countryside. Alleged eyewitness accounts are all chillingly similar. A lonely traveler, out on a cold, dark night suddenly hears the padding of giant paws behind him. He turns to see an enormous black dog materialize out of nowhere and stare at him with glowing red eyes. Most of the time the specter makes no effort to physically harm its victim—at least not right away. The story goes that anyone who sees Black Shuck will die within twelve months.

There are several theories, none of them very comforting, as to how Black Shuck, also known as the Black Dog, got his unique name. Many believe it comes either from the Anglo-Saxon word *scucca*, which means "demon," or from Shukir, the war dog of gods Odin and Thor in Norse mythology. His most infamous appearance was on August 4, 1577, when Black Shuck invaded two Suffolk churches. One was in Bungay, where the hellhound allegedly caused the church tower to collapse, killed two parishioners outright, and caused another to shrivel up "like a drawn purse." The same day he reportedly invaded another church in the nearby town of Blythburgh, leaving scorch marks on the front door that can still be seen today.

Sightings of Black Shuck were reported almost through the present day. During the 1890s, sailors picked up a boy in the open ocean who'd supposedly swum there to escape a demonic dog that was chasing him. In the 1920s and 1930s, fishermen regularly reported hearing the baying of a hound coming from somewhere onshore. And in 1970, British newspapers reported sightings of an unnaturally huge dog bounding along the beach at Great Yarmouth.

Is the local legend in any sense real? Maybe, maybe not. Let's just say that if you're caught out on the moors late at night, it probably can seem very real indeed. The legend certainly fired the interest of novelist Sir Arthur Conan Doyle, who first heard the stories of East Anglia's demon dog in 1901. Doyle, the creator of Sherlock Holmes, had just returned from serving as a field doctor in the Boer War, during which he contracted a persistent fever. Deciding that rest and diversion were the best medicines, he took a golf vacation in Norfolk with a journalist friend named Bertram Fletcher Robinson.

When the two men weren't on the course, they relaxed in comfort at the Royal Links Hotel. There, Robinson acquainted Doyle with the local stories of Black Shuck. The demon dog, he said, liked to run down nearby Mill Lane, right past the very hotel in which they stayed and onto the grounds of nearby Cromer Hall—a place Doyle already knew well, having stayed there as the guest of its master, Lord Cromer.

Not surprisingly, the tale provided useful grist for Doyle's mill. In no time he produced a new Sherlock Holmes novel about a spectral canine that haunts the lives of an illustrious family living in a huge, Gothic home. The family is known to history as the Baskervilles, a name allegedly borrowed from the Cromer family's carriage driver. The novel's four-legged villain got a name change, too—like the book itself, he was called the Hound of the Baskervilles.

LAD

THE DOG WHO BECAME A LITERARY ICON

Today the world's most exalted collie is undoubtedly that wonder dog of TV and film, Lassie. But for a couple of decades at the dawn of the twentieth century, the most well-known member of this four-legged Scottish clan was a male, American-born purebred named Lad. His mostly true adventures were made famous by author Albert Payson Terhune, without doubt the greatest writer ever to devote himself almost exclusively to collies.

Terhune was born into a moneyed, privileged New Jersey family. Originally a newspaper journalist, he soon retired to Sunnybank, the family's summer estate in Wayne, New Jersey. There he acquired Lad, the first and, by his own estimation, most remarkable of the many collies he would own during his life. Terhune wrote that his friend "had a heart that did not know the meaning of fear or disloyalty or of meanness. He was immeasurably more than a professionally loyal and heroic collie. He had the elfin sense of fun and the most human-like reasoning powers I have found in any dog."

Lad, who was born in 1902, lived for sixteen years before passing away in 1918. One year later, Terhune published a memoir of sorts—a collection of short stories called *Lad: A Dog*. The book became a bestseller, and remains in print today. Nowadays, with everything concerning collies overshadowed by Lassie, it's interesting to recall that several generations of children were raised on tales of Lad. A *Peanuts* comic strip once mentioned that the only stories Snoopy wanted read to him were those by Terhune. And in the 1960s TV series *Please Don't Eat the Daisies*, the family sheepdog was facetiously named Ladadog.

It's safe to say that Terhune's work helped elevate the rough collie from just another dog breed into the very symbol of canine heroism, intelligence, and fortitude. Even prior to Terhune's death in 1942, Sunnybank had become a place of pilgrimage for dog lovers from around the world. Today, generations after its owner's passing, the estate remains a public monument. Thousands of visitors stop by every year to visit the graves of Terhune's beloved collies, including that of Lad. It sits off by itself, located on what was, in life, the dog's favorite sleeping spot.

OTHER CANINES OF DISTINCTION

SHARIK: The dog who befriended Russian author Fyodor Dostoevsky during his imprisonment; he was described in Memoirs from the House of the Dead.

TOBY: The pet Rottweiler of artist Sandra Darling (a.k.a. Alexandra Day), he served as the inspiration (and the model) for the "Carl" series of children's books.

LAUTH: A Newfoundland owned by Peter Pan *author J. M. Barrie. He inspired the character of Nana the Newfoundland, who looks after the Darling children.*

PIMPERL: Mozart's Pomeranian, to whom he dedicated an aria.

MARTHA: Paul McCartney's sheepdog and the inspiration for the song "Martha My Dear" on the Beatles' White Album.

POPULAR
CULTURE

OLD DRUM

THE DOG WHO WAS MAN'S FIRST BEST FRIEND

In front of the Johnson County courthouse in Warrensburg, Missouri, stands a bronze statue commemorating an all-but-forgotten dog named Old Drum. But though the hound in question isn't exactly a household name, the eulogy delivered to commemorate his demise gave rise to one of history's most famous canine-related phrases.

The story begins on October 18, 1869—the night Old Drum met his untimely end. The trusted friend and hunting companion of a farmer named Charles Burden, Old Drum was shot and killed by Samuel Ferguson when he strayed onto the property of Ferguson's uncle, Leonidas Hornsby. Hornsby (who was also the brother-in-law of Old Drum's owner) had lost some sheep to marauding canines and vowed to shoot the first stray dog he caught on his land. Unfortunately for Drum, it happened to be him.

Burden, who considered Old Drum a friend rather than a possession, was beside himself. Refusing to let bygones be bygones, he sued Hornsby for damages. The case wended its way through three trials before it was finally settled on September 23, 1870, at the Court of Common Pleas in Warrensburg. Burden brought in one of the biggest guns in

Missouri jurisprudence to plead his case: George Graham Vest, a soon-to-be U.S. senator who was as talented at oratory as he was skilled in the law. When Vest closed his arguments with a stirring "eulogy" for the deceased dog, there wasn't a dry eye in the courthouse—especially on the jury, which found in favor of the still-bereft Burden.

What sealed the deal? Perhaps it was Vest's elegant turn of phrase. Among the many complimentary things he said about Old Drum in particular and dogs in general, he offered this shining sentence: "The one absolutely unselfish friend that man can have in this selfish world, the one that never deserts him and the one that never proves ungrateful or treacherous is his dog." Vest, in his roundabout way, coined the phrase "man's best friend."

The winning speech earned Burden a fairly substantial $50 in damages. Ironically, Old Drum's killer, Samuel Ferguson, was himself gunned down and killed a few years later in Oklahoma.

HACHIKO

THE LOYAL DOG WHO BECAME A JAPANESE LANDMARK

For decades, one of the most popular meeting places for train travelers passing through Tokyo's Shibuya Station has been the Shibuya Hachikoguchi exit. The spot is the site of a famous statue of Hachiko, a large Akita who is famous in Japan for his faithfulness. For years, at pretty much the same spot that his bronze likeness now occupies, Hachiko waited patiently for his beloved master—a master who could never return to him.

The dog who would become a legend was once the pet of Eisaburo Ueno, a professor at the University of Tokyo's department of agriculture. Every workday morning Hachiko would accompany him to Shibuya Station, and every day at 3:00 P.M. he would sit quietly on the landing, awaiting his return. But one day in May 1925, the professor fell ill at work and died suddenly. That afternoon, the loyal Hachiko waited dutifully at his usual spot, only to be disappointed when his master failed to step off the train. Disappointed—but not deterred.

For the next eleven years, Hachiko returned to the platform every day at three o'clock, hoping against hope to catch sight of the professor. The dog became a fixture at the station and was even given sleeping quarters in a storeroom. Eventually the story of the dog reached the newspapers, and Hachiko became a national icon. A popular children's story was based on his life, and in 1934, a bronze statue of him was erected at Shibuya Station. Interestingly, Hachiko himself was on hand for the unveiling. The old dog, in spite of his fame, would keep his lonely vigil until his death on March 8, 1935.

During World War II, the original statue was melted down for use in the Japanese war effort, but a new statue was unveiled in exactly the same spot in 1948, created by the son of the artist who struck the original. Today Hachiko's likeness still waits for his beloved master, unaware that his lonely vigil had important repercussions for his breed. During his lifetime, the Akita was sliding toward extinction. Now, thanks in part to the fame of its best-known representative, it is the national dog of Japan. Hachiko lives on in books and films, and can even be seen, stuffed, at the National Science Museum in Tokyo.

ASHLEY WHIPPET

THE MICHAEL JORDAN OF FRISBEE DOGS

Dogs have chased Frisbees ever since the plastic discs were invented, but it took the work of one exceptional dog to turn this afternoon pastime into a bona fide sport.

The canine in question was named Ashley Whippet. Born on June 4, 1971, Ashley was acquired by Ohio State University (OSU) student Alex Stein when he was just a puppy. Allegedly named after the Ashley Wilkes character in *Gone With the Wind*, with a surname of Whippet because he was, in fact, of the whippet breed, the dog began pursuing Frisbees around the OSU campus at the age of six months. Although other dogs did the same thing, Ashley did it with tremendous élan—streaking after the discs at thirty-five miles per hour (56 km/h), leaping an unbelievable nine feet (3 m) into the air to catch them, and contorting his body into artful, crowd-pleasing poses as he did so. The dog drew audiences wherever he went.

Stein decided to move to Hollywood and get Ashley into show business. Talent agents wouldn't give the pooch the time of day, so the duo took a more direct approach. On August 5, 1974, the Los Angeles Dodgers were set to host the Cincinnati

Reds in front of a national TV audience. Stein bought a ticket and smuggled Ashley into the stadium. At the bottom of the eighth inning, just before the Dodgers came to bat, he and his dog sprinted out to centerfield and started an impromptu round of fetch. The crowd was so amazed that the game ground to a halt. Announcer Joe Garagiola, who was supposed to be talking about baseball, did "play by play" for the dog instead.

For his trouble, Stein was fined $250 and arrested for trespassing. But the dose of national exposure turned Ashley into a canine sports hero. He appeared on *The Tonight Show*, *Monday Night Football*, and even during halftime at Super Bowl XII. In 1975 the World Frisbee Championships (previously an all-human affair) inaugurated a "Catch and Fetch" competition for canines—an event Ashley won three years in a row. He so dominated the event that in 1982 it was renamed the Ashley Whippet Invitational. Though Ashley passed on in March 1985, the contest that bears his name still attracts thousands of canine participants.

RIN TIN TIN

THE DOG WHO SAVED A MOVIE STUDIO

Many dogs are famous for saving individual lives. But one canine was responsible for rescuing an entire company. This honor belongs to the legendary German shepherd Rin Tin Tin, the four-legged big-screen star whose box office receipts single-handedly saved Warner Bros. from ruin.

It was a miracle that the studio's savior even survived his puppyhood. The dog who would become a celebrity was born in France at the end of World War I, inside an abandoned, bombed-out kennel. United States Army Corporal Lee Duncan found him starving there along with his mother and his four littermates. Duncan, a dog lover, found homes for the mother and three of the pups, but he kept a male and a female for himself. He named them after two French puppet characters: Nanette and Rin Tin Tin.

Nanette died from distemper shortly after she and her brother traveled with Duncan to his Los Angeles home. Duncan worked at a hardware store to make ends meet and spent his spare time training Rin Tin Tin. Convinced that his furry friend had a big future in show business, he wrote a script for him called *Where the North Begins* and offered it and Rin Tin Tin (nicknamed Rinny) to any studio exec who would give them the time of day.

As it turned out, none of them would. Duncan was turned down again and again. Then, one afternoon, he and Rinny happened to spot a film crew trying to shoot a scene that featured an extremely uncooperative wolf. Duncan offered his dog's services, promising that he could do whatever was asked of him in one take. After much jawboning, the crew decided to give the newcomer a shot. Rinny, as promised, delivered a perfect performance on the first try. A star was born.

Rin Tin Tin became the canine lead of the film, called *Man from Hell's River*. It was a huge hit for its studio, Warner Bros.—though "studio" was perhaps too grandiose a name for a shoestring operation consisting of a handful of employees, a few cameras, and four immigrant brothers from Poland named Harry, Albert, Sam, and Jack Warner. Rin Tin Tin would make twenty-six pictures for the company over the next decade, becoming both a wonder dog and a cash cow. At studio headquarters, no one doubted that the only thing keeping the wolf from the door was the work of a single, very talented German shepherd—a German shepherd who was fondly referred to around the water cooler as "the mortgage lifter."

At one time Rinny was as big a name as any to be found today on Hollywood Boulevard's Walk of Fame—the dog received some ten thousand pieces of fan mail during his heyday. He kept working until he died unexpectedly on Friday, August 10, 1932. The following Monday he'd been scheduled to start shooting his next film.

Rin Tin Tin's progeny attempted to continue his legacy. A son, dubbed Rin Tin Tin II, briefly carried on in films. During World War II another son, Rin Tin Tin III, joined Duncan in training some five thousand canines and their human handlers as war dogs. But Rin Tin Tin's true legacy resides on the silver screen. Without him, Warner Bros. would have gone under—and such Warner Bros. classics as *Casablanca* and *Rebel Without a Cause* might never have been made.

GREYFRIARS BOBBY

THE TINY DOG WHO BECAME A TOWERING MONUMENT TO LOYALTY

The ancient Scottish cemetery known as Greyfriars Kirkyard (churchyard) has accepted tenants for hundreds of years. Today the Edinburgh landmark serves as the final resting place for many great names, but none can match the fame of a humble dog known as Bobby, whose devotion to his deceased master made him an undying symbol of fidelity.

The saga of Greyfriars Bobby began around 1856, when a gardener named John Gray moved to Edinburgh with his family and took a job as a night watchman. To keep him company on patrols, he took along his tiny, furry Skye terrier, Bobby. The two were inseparable and became a fixture on the city's streets. But years of walking his beat in all kinds of weather took their toll on Gray, who contracted tuberculosis and died in 1858. He was buried in Greyfriars Kirkyard.

Bobby refused to accept his companion's passing. He began to frequent the cemetery, never straying far from Gray's grave, in spite of the cemetery's staff energetic efforts to evict him. Finally, his devotion won the hearts of the local citizenry. A shelter was erected for Bobby close to his master's final resting place, and the terrier was given regular meals at a nearby coffeehouse where he and his master had once dined together. As his fame grew, tourists would gather at the entrance of the churchyard around 1 P.M., waiting for Bobby to march, like clockwork, from the cemetery to the restaurant.

The faithful dog kept his vigil until his own death on January 14, 1872, at the age of sixteen. Because canines were forbidden burial on consecrated ground, he was given a grave near the churchyard's entrance. His headstone reads: "Greyfriars Bobby, died 14th January 1872, aged 16 years. Let his loyalty and devotion be a lesson

to us all."

The headstone's inscription seems to ring true. Almost a century and a half have passed since Bobby's departure, but his deeds live on. In 1873 a bronze sculpture of the loyal canine—modeled from the original, still-living Bobby—was raised just outside the entrance to Greyfriars Kirkyard. The coffee shop where the little dog and his master took their meals is still in business. It is now called, simply, Greyfriars Bobby.

PICKLES

THE DOG WHO RESCUED THE WORLD CUP

The 1966 World Cup is fondly remembered for exploits both on and off the soccer field. Held in Great Britain, it featured an unexpected tournament victory by the home team. But the off-court antics were even more riveting. Before the tournament, the priceless Jules Rimet Trophy, which was traditionally awarded to the winning team, was stolen—and it might never have been found, if not for the curious nose of a mutt named Pickles.

Three months before the World Cup was set to begin, the trophy was placed on display at Central Hall in Westminster, London. A team of guards was supposed to watch it at all times, because it was very valuable—both for sentimental reasons and because the piece, made of gold-plated sterling silver and set with lapis lazuli, was worth a small fortune. Yet, somehow, on March 20, 1966, someone managed to pry open the case in which it was housed and make off with it.

The theft ignited an international media firestorm and triggered a massive manhunt. A ransom note for £15,000 arrived, and a police sting led to the capture of the man who authored it. However, he claimed to be only an intermediary for the real thief, whom he knew only as "The

Pole." In spite of intense questioning, the man responsible for the ransom note refused to give up the cup before the police offered him a deal on prison time and privileges.

As it turned out, the authorities didn't need his cooperation. A week later, as David Corbett, a resident of Norwood, South London, was out for a walk with his dog, Pickles, the canine found a newspaper-wrapped package under a garden hedge. Corbett pulled it out, tore off the wrapping, and found a statue of a woman holding a dish over her head—a woman who appeared to be made of gold. Being a soccer fan, he instantly realized his dog had found the World Cup.

Pickles became an overnight celebrity and even got to attend the victory party for the British team. Corbett used the reward money from the discovery to buy a house. However, the Jules Rimet Trophy refused to stay found. In 1983 it was stolen in Rio de Janeiro, and hasn't been seen since.

NIPPER

THE DOG WHO BECAME ONE OF THE WORLD'S MOST FAMOUS ADVERTISING LOGOS

Some company logos, such as the Nike "swoosh" and the Mercedes-Benz three-pointed star, are known around the world. But few corporate symbols are as enduring, or as loved, as the one featuring a mixed-breed British dog named Nipper staring at an old-fashioned record player. For more than a century, this picture, called "His Master's Voice," has been one of advertising's most indelible images.

It all began in 1887 when British artist Francis Barraud inherited a small, mixed-breed dog named Nipper (because he nipped people's legs). The dog came from the estate of his deceased brother, Mark, along with an Edison Bell cylinder phonograph that included some recordings of his late brother's voice. Nipper lived with the artist and his family until his own passing in 1895. Several years later, in 1898, Barraud executed a painting of Nipper listening curiously to his master's voice on the cylinder phonograph. The piece, originally titled *Dog Looking at and Listening to a Phonograph*, was shopped around to various recording firms, but to no avail.

Frustrated, Barraud changed the painting's name to the catchier *His Master's Voice*. Finally, in 1899, the new Gramaphone Company decided to buy all rights to the work—but only if the artist replaced the Edison machine in the original painting with a more modern-looking model. The artist complied and was paid fifty pounds for the painting and another fifty for the full copyright. The picture was used in various advertising pieces and became an immediate success. In a few years it found its way onto all of Gramaphone's new releases and became so ubiquitous that the company, though it never officially changed its name, became known as HMV (short for His Master's Voice).

The symbol became even bigger in the United States, where rights to the image were acquired by the Victor Talking Machine Company, which plastered it on all of their records. Nipper became so intimately associated with the company that their magazine advertisements told buyers to "Look for the dog." Today Nipper's reputation still looms large. In the United States he's strongly associated with Victor's corporate successor, RCA. In Europe, the company that eventually acquired Gramaphone, EMI, now uses Nipper to promote its line of retail stores, appropriately called HMV.

STRONGHEART

THE FIRST GERMAN SHEPHERD MOVIE STAR

These days Rin Tin Tin is the only canine silent film star that most people remember. But another German shepherd, Strongheart, had his name up in lights years earlier.

His owner, animal trainer Larry Trimble, had set out to create a star. In 1920 he began a careful search for an animal with movie idol pizzazz. He found just what he was looking for in Germany, where he met a powerful, 125-pound (57 kg), three-year-old attack dog named Etzel von Oringer. The dog was more comfortable biting people than doing scenes with them, but Trimble saw something he liked in Etzel. He changed the canine's name to the more marquee-friendly Strongheart and brought him to Hollywood.

It took months of training to take the edge off the dog's suspicious, police-dog personality, but in time Trimble succeeded in transforming Strongheart from a dangerous fighting machine into a friendly, loving pet and budding thespian. Interestingly, one trait from his days in law enforcement never left Strongheart—the dog could size up the character of strangers unerringly and made a habit of glaring at, and even stalking, those he didn't trust.

His first movie, 1921's *The Silent Call*, instantly

turned the German shepherd into a four-legged action hero. Just like a human star, he made personal appearances all over the country, where his fans lined up for a chance to have a look and, perhaps, to pat his enormous head.

During the 1920s Strongheart made film after film, with titles such as *Brawn of the North* and *The Return of Boston Blackie*. He even developed a romantic interest with a female German shepherd named Lady Jule. The two appeared together onscreen, and offscreen they produced several litters of puppies.

Strongheart's movie career came to a tragic end in the summer of 1929. While doing a stunt for his next project, the normally sure-footed dog slipped and fell into a hot studio light. The resulting burn refused to heal, and it claimed his life a few weeks later. But his legacy lived on in surprising ways: His numerous offspring starred in several films, the Strongheart dog food brand is named after him, and perhaps most importantly, he's one of only three canines (along with Rin Tin Tin and Lassie) to earn a star on the Hollywood Walk of Fame.

PAL

THE REAL DOG BEHIND LASSIE, THE WORLD'S GREATEST CANINE CELEBRITY

Everybody knows Lassie, but far fewer know the dog who first played her on screen. And yet Pal, who portrayed the world's smartest collie in the seminal 1943 film *Lassie Come Home*, has an interesting story to share. Despite his early days as an incorrigible obedience school dropout, this undeniably male dog became an international sensation by portraying a female canine.

Lassie was "born" in 1938, when author Eric Knight penned a short story for the *Saturday Evening Post* called *Lassie Come-Home*, about a collie who travels the length of Scotland to reunite with the boy she loves. The popular tale became an even more popular novel, and in 1943 MGM signed it up as a movie. An elite show collie was engaged to play the title role, but fate intervened when northern California's Sacramento River flooded, providing a once-in-a-lifetime chance to get some spectacular footage of "Lassie" fording the water. However, the canine thespian the studio cast was still in training and wasn't ready to begin filming. MGM turned to a company called Weatherwax Trained Dogs, run by brothers Rudd and Frank Weatherwax, for a stand-in.

To say that the brothers were a little low on collies at the time would be an understatement. The dog the brothers offered the studio was a male named Pal. His original owner couldn't train him properly and had turned to the Weatherwaxes for help; when the man found he couldn't pay the ten dollars he owed the brothers for their work, he surrendered the dog as payment instead. Pal was no one's idea of a show dog. He lacked the "classic" collie look and had a penchant for chasing cars, but he did have one key advantage—he could act.

The Weatherwax brothers and the film crew discovered just how good he was at the bank of the Sacramento River. Pal didn't just ford the river on cue. When he emerged onto the bank, he appeared exhausted, as if barely able to drag himself onto dry land. In acting parlance, he nailed it. From that moment on, Pal was a star. As MGM studio head Louis B. Mayer reportedly said when he saw the footage, "Pal had entered the water, but Lassie had come out."

OSCAR

THE DOG WHO BECAME AN INTERNET CELEBRITY

In the digital age, worldwide fame comes quickly and easily. Even dogs can do it.

One such canine Internet sensation was manufactured in 2006. The dog in question owed its celebrity to a bizarre class assignment at Adcenter, the graduate advertising program at Virginia Commonwealth University. Mike Lear, one of the program's adjunct professors, asked his class to help make his pug, Oscar, famous.

The idea was to use viral marketing to turn the diminutive dog into a big deal. Some students put up flyers, while others created pug-intensive rap songs. But someone else (no one's ever figured out who) took it to the next level. He or she posted an anonymous announcement on the social networking site Myspace.com stating that Oscar would be killed online.

That did the trick. The story spread worldwide. Animal lovers bombarded the university with irate messages, and eventually the police looked into the matter. Oscar, just as the assignment outlined, was a star. However, the project's original instructions stated that no threats of harm could be made against the pug. "Whoever did it got an F," Adcenter managing director Rick Boyko told the *Richmond Times-Dispatch*.

GRIGIO

THE DOG WHO BECAME A SAINT'S GUARDIAN ANGEL

Tales of Catholic saints regularly include stories of divine intervention, but Saint Giovanni Melchior Bosco (better known as Don Bosco) enjoyed protection that was a little more down-to-earth: a gigantic dog-turned-bodyguard named Grigio.

Bosco, who lived from 1815 to 1888, spent his life helping underprivileged boys in and around the industrial town of Turin, Italy. During the early days of his ministry he was in danger both from criminals, who thought he had money to steal, and businessmen and city officials, who resented his attempts to organize and educate their low-cost labor pool. Over the years, Don Bosco survived several determined attempts on his life. And they might have succeeded, were it not for the repeated—and nearly inexplicable—interventions of the enormous Grigio. When Bosco was in danger, the huge dog would appear out of nowhere to rout his attackers. Once order was restored, he'd simply turn and walk away.

As the years passed and Bosco's reputation grew, neither thieves nor local officials dared to touch him. And the mighty Grigio, who was always drawn by trouble, simply faded away, never to be seen again.

BOBBIE

THE DOG WHO TRAVELED 2,500 MILES TO REUNITE WITH HIS FAMILY

The famous movie *Lassie Come Home* tells the story of an intrepid collie who walks the length of Scotland to find the boy she loves. But even that legendary journey sounds like a mere walk around the block when compared to the real-life accomplishments of an American collie named Bobbie. To reunite with his family, Bobbie undertook a half-year, 2,500-mile (4,000 km) journey across the breadth of the continental United States.

Bobbie began his life as the companion of G. F. Brazier, a restaurant owner in Silverton, Oregon. During the summer of 1923, Brazier, his wife, and Bobbie traveled to Indiana by car. There, during a stopover in the tiny town of Wolcott, the couple lost track of their dog. Figuring he was gone forever, they resumed their journey.

As the weeks passed, the memories of Bobbie faded. But six months later, on February 15, 1924, something truly miraculous happened. Brazier's stepdaughter, Nova, was walking down a Silverton street when she spotted a skinny, shaggy collie who nevertheless looked a lot like the long-lost Bobbie. She commented on the resemblance to a companion, and the dog, hearing the word

"Bobbie," rushed to the delighted girl, danced around her, and smothered her with kisses. Bobbie soon was reunited with his entire family, which identified him beyond all doubt by several old scars and other marks the dog had acquired while living with them.

No one could imagine how the dog managed to travel so far—or how he'd even known where to go. But as the story of Bobbie the Wonder Dog (as he came to be known) spread around the nation, people who had helped him along the way wrote the Braziers to tell what happened. Apparently the dog had retraced, almost exactly, the route the family took to Indiana. "He would turn up at some house where we had stopped or some town we had passed through, his eyes half closed and red with strain, his feet bleeding, ravenously hungry, so tired he was ready to drop," Brazier wrote in a contemporary account. "Some friend of dogs would feed and doctor him and he would rest for a while, but as soon as he could, he would be up and away again."

When he arrived at a spot he recognized from his car trip, Bobbie's first order of business was to frantically run from room to room, looking for his lost family. He would take no notice of the people who actually lived or worked in the place until after he'd satisfied himself that his human companions were nowhere present. His diligence, not to mention his phenomenal navigational skills, turned him into a media darling. Books were written about him, he made numerous personal appearances, and his exploits were recounted in a movie. An Oregon contractor built Bobbie his own "dream" doghouse—a miniature bungalow equipped with eight curtained windows. He was also the guest of honor at a Portland exposition, where he was petted by more than 100,000 fans.

Today the fame of Bobbie the Wonder Dog lives on in his hometown of Silverton, where his February 15 return date is commemorated as Bobbie Day. There's a statue of the famous canine, a mural recounting his exploits, and even a replica of the deluxe doghouse he got for finding his way home.

TOGO AND BALTO

THE DOGS WHO HELPED SAVE A CITY FROM A PLAGUE

The Iditarod Trail Sled Dog Race, held every spring in Alaska, is considered one of the world's most grueling sporting events. Teams of sled dogs traverse the state's frozen wastes, covering some 1,100 miles (1,770 km) in eight to fifteen days. The contest was created to commemorate an even more grueling event—the 1925 serum run to Nome. That legendary achievement was no mere race for a trophy; it was a race for life itself. And without the selfless service of dozens of great, and two *really* great, sled dogs, it might well have been lost.

The saga began in the winter of 1925, when a potentially deadly diphtheria epidemic threatened the far northern town of Nome. The nearest supply of antitoxin was more than a thousand miles (1,610 km) away in Anchorage. With no trustworthy road connection, train, or aircraft service and a bitter Arctic winter in progress, the tiny spot on the map was as isolated as if it were on the moon.

Only one form of transportation seemed up to the challenge—dogsled. The twenty-pound (9 kg) container of serum was taken north by rail to the town of Nenana, which was literally the end of the line. Then, on the night of January 27, it was handed over to the first of almost two dozen "mushers," charged with carrying it safely, over 674 miles (1,085 km) of snow-covered, viciously cold tundra, to the citizens of Nome.

More than one hundred dogs participated in the serum run, but two stand out. The first and greatest was Togo, a massive Siberian husky who led the sled team of musher Leonhard Seppala. Togo was up to the task, to say the least. The forty-eight-pound (22 kg) canine and his team had to travel 170 miles (274 km) in three days just to reach the spot on the route where they picked up the serum. Then the dogs covered the most difficult stretch of the course, traveling in near-white-out conditions and gale-force winds that gave the air a wind chill of negative seventy degrees Fahrenheit (-57°C). Seppala became hopelessly disoriented and relied on Togo to keep the sled on the seemingly invisible trail. As Togo led the group across the treacherous, ice-covered Norton Sound, they became trapped on a piece of ice that broke away from the rest of the thick ice sheet. While still wearing his leather harness and traces, Togo leaped five feet (1.5 m) to solid ice so he could pull the sled to safety. Togo's harness broke during the attempt, but he used his teeth to retrieve it from the icy water. Grasping the leather traces in his jaws, he then pulled the floe to the ice sheet so Seppala, the sled, and the other dogs could proceed. Togo gave every last bit of his strength to the effort, and was lamed for life in the process.

About fifty miles (80 km) outside of Nome, the serum was handed over to a fresh sled team, led by a dog named Balto. This was the canine who brought the medicine to the stricken town and became a celebrity. A famous statue of Balto was even erected in New York City's Central Park in 1925.

Those in the know, however, considered Seppala and Togo to be the true heroes. And though he played second fiddle to Balto, Togo created a legacy far more lasting than any mere statue. After retiring from sledding, he became one of the founding sires of the modern Siberian husky line. Though he died in 1929, his strength and intelligence live on in his legion of descendants.

JOSEPHINE

THE DOG WHO LAUNCHED JACQUELINE SUSANN'S WRITING CAREER

Jacqueline Susann is remembered for two things—becoming the first "celebrity novelist" by relentlessly promoting her books on TV talk shows, and for writing *Valley of the Dolls*, a trashy show business tell-all that sold an unprecedented 20 million copies, making it one of the most popular novels of all time.

But the work of the world's greatest pulp fiction writer might never have seen print were it not for her poodle, Josephine. Susann acquired the dog in 1955, when she resided in New York City and made her living on the lowest links of the show business food chain. She wanted to be a writer, and even had an idea for a novel about starlets who have their lives destroyed by illicit drugs and sex—but no one would give her the time of day. So instead she served up a funny, semi-true memoir about her relationship with her poodle, whom she often dressed in outfits that matched her own. Published in 1963, *Every Night, Josephine!* was a modest success. It gave Susann enough clout to get *Dolls* printed—and the rest, as they say, is publishing history.

HANDSOME DAN

THE WORLD'S FIRST COLLEGE MASCOT

Back in 1889, when Yale University unveiled a bulldog named Handsome Dan, the idea of a live animal representing a school was quite new. Dan, an enormous, muscle-bound bulldog, certainly seemed perfect for the job. Purchased for five dollars from a local blacksmith, he was the very embodiment of the never-say-die spirit coveted by sports teams. According to one contemporary observer, he looked "like a cross between an alligator and a horned frog."

The first Dan, who delighted fans with his near-pathological hatred of anyone decked in Harvard crimson, stayed on the job until his death in 1898. Yet his legacy lives on. More than a dozen "Handsome Dans" have held his post since then, with varying degrees of success. Several were "retired" when they were found to be afraid of crowds, and one developed the unfortunate but highly amusing habit of attacking the mascots of opposing teams. Fans of the original Handsome Dan can still see his preserved body, in all its glowering glory, inside a glass display case at Yale's Payne Whitney Gymnasium.

GUNTHER IV

THE DOG WHO BECAME A REAL-ESTATE MOGUL

Several years ago the British tabloid the *Sun* ran a list of the world's ten richest pets—a decidedly rarified roster consisting of various nonhumans who inherited millions from their loving but deceased owners. Topping all the rest was a German shepherd named Gunther IV. The dog was allegedly worth about $100 million—an inheritance from his father, Gunther III, who received the cash in 1992 in the will of his dear departed mistress, a German countess named Karlotta Liebenstein.

Various newspapers called this story into question, wondering whether the whole thing was some sort of bizarre hoax. But Gunther IV, who regularly appeared in public, really seemed to have a great deal of cash behind him. On November 11, 2002, Gunther (and two members of his "staff") turned up at an auction in Italy, where he—through intermediaries, of course—paid three million lira for a rare truffle.

Gunther IV made his biggest waves in the Miami Beach real estate market. In 1999 the mainstream press was filled with reports that he—or rather, his acquisitive human associates—were negotiating to purchase Sylvester Stallone's beachfront estate for a reported $25 million. Failing at that, the dog and his two-legged flunkies plunked down $7.5 million for Madonna's former Miami residence. According to Gunther's Web site, the lucky dog moved into the Material Girl's master suite, while the rest of the house was taken over by his companions—a mysterious group of five twentysomething humans called "the Burgundians."

And therein hangs a tail. Or rather, tale. Described online as "five euphoric young people," the Burgundians looked like severely over-tanned Eurotrash—but that wasn't the full story. They were, apparently, a severely over-tanned Eurotrash *pop group*. Gunther served as the front "man" for a collection of international investors intent on turning the three girls and two boys into a singing sensation. How this agenda was advanced by having them consort with a rich German shepherd is anybody's guess, but their money was for real, even if the story about Gunther inheriting it was made up. At last report, Gunther was still enjoying his stay in Madonna's master suite. No word on what happened to the Burgundians.

BLUE

HOCKEY'S SCARIEST DOG

Sports commentator and former NHL coach Don Cherry is a Canadian national icon. A longtime regular on the television sports show *Hockey Night in Canada*, he rose to fame in the 1970s as head coach of the Boston Bruins. During his three-year tenure with the team, Cherry developed a reputation for eccentricity and flamboyancy. He was also a great fan of "physical" (by which he meant combative) play. It's even been said (and Cherry has never denied) that he modeled the team's playing style after the take-no-prisoners attitude of his female English bull terrier, Blue.

Today Cherry is a media phenomenon, and so is the latest Blue—the ex-coach has owned a line of bull terriers, all with the same name. The two appear together regularly, and Blue is even featured during the opening of Cherry's *Hockey Night* appearances. In one famous incident, chronicled in the Canadian news magazine *Maclean's*, the combative canine once took a bite out of Cherry's wife, Rose. When one of his friends suggested he should "get rid of her," the coach replied, "Me and Blue'll sure miss her."

JIM

THE DOG WHO HAD A PARK NAMED AFTER HIM

Dedicating an entire park to a dog is a one-in-a-million event, so the canine it honors had better be a one-in-a-million dog. That was certainly the case for a Llewelyn setter named Jim. In 1999, sixty-two years after his death, Jim's hometown of Marshall, Missouri, honored him by opening Jim the Wonder Dog Memorial Park.

Jim's full name goes a long way toward explaining why he rates his own stretch of greenery in the heart of town. Born on March 10, 1925, to a Louisiana dog breeder, he was acquired by Missouri resident Sam Van Arsdale, who trained him for quail hunting. Jim proved a quick study but seemed otherwise unremarkable. That is, until a fall day several years later, when man and dog were out hunting together. According to legend, Van Arsdale absently said to Jim, "Let's sit in the shade of that hickory tree and rest." The dog promptly trotted over to the hickory tree and sat down.

Intrigued, Van Arsdale then allegedly asked Jim to find an oak tree. Which he did. He also, in rapid succession, picked out a walnut tree, a cedar tree, and several other examples of the local flora, guided only by verbal cues.

Not long afterward, Jim switched vocations

from gun dog to publicity hound. In no time fans started traveling hundreds of miles to the town of Marshall to see the wonder dog in action. They were rarely disappointed. Repeatedly, he seemed to demonstrate the ability to understand commands in any language, from German to Greek—languages of which his master, Van Arsdale, had no knowledge. He could locate specific cars based on their license plate numbers, pick individuals out of crowds based solely on physical descriptions, and "read" written messages. Jim performed before a joint session of the Missouri state legislature and at the University of Missouri before a panel of professors. They told the assembled crowd, according to *Rural Missouri* magazine, that "Jim possessed an occult power that might never come again to a dog in many generations."

No wonder some people semiseriously claimed him to be the reincarnation of King Solomon.

But the talents of the innocuous-looking dog didn't end there. Jim could reportedly unerringly pick the sexes of unborn babies, and he was a wiz at calling sporting events. Among his many other feats, he allegedly divined the winner of the Kentucky Derby seven years in a row and selected the Yankees to win the 1936 World Series (which they did). During a trip to Florida, bettors actually threatened him with death if he didn't stop picking winners at a local dog track. After that, Van Arsdale became so afraid of gambling interests stealing his dog that he kept him close to home, refusing an offer for him to make movies at Paramount and to shill for a dog food company.

By the time of his death on March 18, 1937, Jim the Wonder Dog was one of the world's most famous canines. Van Arsdale wanted him buried in the family plot at Ridge Park Cemetery. When local regulations wouldn't permit it, the earthly remains of the world's smartest dog were interred in a specially made casket just outside the gate. Over the years the cemetery expanded around the spot, so now Jim lies well within hallowed ground. Fans still visit his grave—and far more stop by downtown's Jim the Wonder Dog Memorial Park, the centerpiece of which is a life-size statue of the brilliant canine.

OTHER CANINES OF DISTINCTION

SPUDS MACKENZIE: A four-legged shill for Bud Light. This distinctive bull terrier (who was actually a female named Honey Tree Evil Eye) debuted in a 1987 Super Bowl commercial. Ironically, "Spuds" died of kidney failure in 1993.

LITTLE DUKE: An Airedale who was the childhood pet of Marion Robert Morrison, the man who would become John Wayne, a.k.a. "The Duke." Wayne got his nickname as a boy, when neighbors started referring to him as "Big Duke" to differentiate him from his canine companion.

BUMMER AND LAZARUS: Two stray dogs who were the talk of San Francisco in the early 1860s. They were so popular that their adventures were regularly published in the local papers.

LUCKY: The official mascot of The National Enquirer *during its heyday in the 1970s.*

TEDDY: A Great Dane who appeared in many Max Sennet comedies and was the first canine movie star in the United States.

HEROES

SGT. STUBBY

THE HIGHEST-RANKING DOG IN WORLD WAR I

Many combat dogs have been drafted into military service. Some are yanked from their civilian homes and into the armed forces, while others are raised from puppyhood for duty on the front lines. But the brown-and-white American pit bull terrier known as Stubby was strictly a volunteer. The bedraggled dog, who got his name because of his abbreviated tail, was found as a puppy by U.S. Army Private John Robert Conroy when he was training for deployment in Europe during World War I. Stubby soon became a boot camp favorite. He even learned to "salute" by raising his right paw to his right eyebrow.

Stubby accompanied Conroy's unit, the 102nd Infantry Division, when they shipped out for France. But his comrades in arms soon discovered Stubby was far more than a mere mascot. One night, when his sensitive nose detected a surprise poison gas attack, he saved numberless lives by running through the trenches, barking and tugging at sleeping soldiers. He also patrolled no-man's land, sniffing out wounded troops and either summoning help or personally leading them to safety. On one occasion he surprised and captured a German forward observer who was attempting to spy on allied defensive positions. Stubby flushed him from behind a bush, chased him down, and clamped the soldier's backside firmly in his jaws—a grip he resolutely maintained until men from his unit arrived to take charge of the prisoner. For his actions that day, the commander of the 102nd awarded the dog the rank of sergeant.

Stubby participated in more than a dozen battles, surviving everything from repeated poison gas attacks to an uncomfortably close encounter with a hand grenade. He returned to the United States with Conroy, where he received a hero's welcome. He met President Woodrow Wilson, was inducted into the American Legion, and received a Humane Society medal from his "supreme commander," Gen. Joseph "Black Jack" Pershing, the leader of the American Expeditionary Forces during the war. But best of all, he was allowed to retire from the military with Conroy, with whom he lived happily—and peacefully—until his death in 1926.

BELLE

THE DOG WHO DIALED 911

Over the centuries, countless dogs have summoned assistance for their stricken owners. But few of those canine heroes displayed as much presence of mind—not to mention technical savvy—as an English beagle named Belle. Instead of running for help, she *dialed* for it.

In what was probably the luckiest move of his life, Florida resident Kevin Weaver acquired the diminutive hound from a pet store. Good fortune also smiled on Belle that day, because the feisty dog had already been returned to the store by two previous owners who were dissatisfied with her behavior.

Weaver is a lifelong diabetic who suffers from potentially dangerous seizures if his blood sugar level drops too low. Since he lives alone, he decided to have Belle trained as a medical assistance dog. A nine-month, $9,000 course taught the tiny beagle how to gauge her master's blood sugar level by licking his nose and smelling his breath once each hour. If things seem a bit "off," she whines and paws at Weaver, letting him know that he needs to take action.

This costly, lengthy training regimen paid off on the morning of February 7, 2006. On that fateful day, Weaver awoke feeling woozy. His blood sugar was dangerously low, but he was too befuddled to realize what was wrong. But Belle *did* realize, and grew very agitated. Thinking all she wanted was to go to the bathroom, Weaver escorted her outside. But when the two of them came back indoors, Weaver collapsed on the floor of his kitchen.

He might have died there, had Belle not remembered another important part of her training: In case her master was ever incapacitated, she'd been shown how to dial 911 on a phone by chomping down on the numeral 9, which was programmed to call emergency services. Belle located Weaver's cell phone, then gnawed on the appropriate key until an emergency dispatcher came on the line. The dog barked hysterically into the handset and didn't stop until an ambulance arrived. Weaver was treated in time and made a full recovery. And Belle, needless to say, became a hero. "I am convinced that if Belle wasn't with me that morning, I wouldn't be alive today," Weaver told the Associated Press. "Belle is more than just a lifesaver; she's my best friend."

DORADO

THE DOG WHO SAVED HIS MASTER ON 9/11

The tragedy of 9/11 produced countless examples of courage in the face of danger, but few tales of self-sacrifice and steadfast bravery rival that of Dorado, a four-year-old Labrador retriever. Dorado served as a guide dog for blind computer technician Omar Eduardo Rivera. On the fateful morning of the terrorist attacks, he and his canine companion were working on the seventy-first floor of the World Trade Center's north tower. Dorado was asleep under Rivera's desk.

A hijacked airliner struck the skyscraper twenty-five stories above Rivera's office. Though he wasn't injured, he was soon surrounded by the sounds of panic and the smell of smoke. Fearing that, given his disability, he had no chance of escaping the fire and chaos, Rivera unleashed Dorado (which means "gold" in Spanish), gave him a final pat on the head, and bid him farewell, hoping the dog would find a way to save himself. "Not having any sight, I knew I wouldn't be able to run down the stairs and through all the obstacles like other people," Rivera told the *Contra Costa Times*. "I was resigned to dying and decided to free Dorado and give him a chance to escape. It wasn't fair that we should both die in that hell."

Rivera figured that Dorado would dash for the nearest escape route. But though his master seemed resigned to death, Dorado had other ideas. A couple of minutes after his release, he returned to Rivera's side and started nudging him toward an emergency staircase that was already crammed with fleeing office workers. There, with the aid of Rivera's boss, who happened to pass by at just the right moment, the steadfast dog led Rivera on an hour-long descent down seventy flights to the street. The three then walked several blocks, reaching safety only moments before the tower collapsed behind them. "It was then that I knew for certain he loved me just as much as I loved him," Rivera said. "He was prepared to die in the hope he might save my life. I owe my life to Dorado—my companion and best friend."

BUOY

THE DOG WHO WAS LITERALLY A GUARDIAN ANGEL

Dragica Vlaco owes her life to an act of God—or, more accurately, an act of dog.

It happened on an October evening in 2002, while Jim Simpson hosted a Halloween party at his home in Richland, Washington. Everyone was in costume, including his yellow Labrador retriever, Buoy, who wore a halo and angel's wings. At around 8:30 P.M., Simpson took Buoy, still in costume, out for their typical placid stroll along the Columbia River. But instead of walking quietly, the lab bolted off into the darkness, ignoring his owner's commands to return.

Simpson found Buoy at the river's edge, standing over a soaking wet, shoeless woman who was crawling along on her hands and knees, shivering violently. Simpson summoned help and carried her to his house. The woman, Dragica Vlaco, had taken strong pain medication for a recent shoulder operation, became disoriented, wandered outside, and fell into the frigid river. If it hadn't been for Buoy, she probably would have died of exposure. "He's a pretty friendly dog and pretty curious about people," Simpson told the *Tri-State Herald*. "It's a good thing he went over there."

TIP

THE DOG WHO WAS NO FAIR-WEATHER FRIEND

The folks around the town of Bamford, England, still remember the story of Tip, the devoted companion of eighty-five-year-old Joseph Tagg. Tagg, a retired sheep farmer and sheepdog trainer, bred highly skilled border collies, but no one would understand just how great they were until Tip came along.

On December 12, 1953, the still-spry Tagg set off on a long walk through the nearby moors, but neither he nor his walking partner, Tip, returned. For weeks, rescue teams combed the surrounding countryside, until heavy snow and bitter cold forced an end to the search. Fifteen weeks passed before the body of Tagg, who had apparently expired of natural causes in the middle of his jaunt, was stumbled upon by a couple of locals. They could hardly believe their eyes when they also discovered poor Tip, emaciated and near death, still standing guard over the body.

Tip was nursed back to health, but he survived his master by just a year—long enough, however, for his story to spread worldwide. Today he lies buried on the moors that took Tagg's life, beneath a stone monument that tells his story.

BAMSE

THE SEA DOG WHO BECAME A NORWEGIAN NATIONAL HERO

During World War II, a Saint Bernard named Bamse became the largest dog to serve on an Allied vessel—and possibly the largest dog to serve on any vessel, of any sort, in any age.

The huge dog was the mascot of a tiny minesweeper with a crew of only eighteen men. The vessel, called the *Thorudd* (Whale Catcher), was crewed by Norwegian sailors serving with the Free Norwegian Forces and stationed at the port towns of Montrose and Dundee in Scotland. During his sea service, Bamse (which means "cuddly bear") rescued a crew member from a knife-wielding assailant by shoving the attacker off a dock. When another sailor fell off the *Thorudd* at sea, the enormous Saint Bernard plunged in after him, grabbed a mouthful of his clothing, and towed him to shore.

Bamse was equally courageous in battle. He sat in the vessel's forward gun turret, decked out in a tin helmet, when the tiny ship was at battle stations. Onshore he was equipped with a sailor's hat and a bus pass, so that on weekends he could ride into nearby towns, track down inebriated crewmates, and gently escort them home.

Not surprisingly, the big dog became a local

landmark in Montrose and Dundee and a national hero in Norway. He figured prominently in the tiny country's May 17 Constitution Day, and was featured on a Christmas card dispatched to all Norwegian servicemen.

Sadly, the gentle giant didn't survive the war. On July 22, 1944, he died of unknown causes at dockside, with his crewmates at his side. The death of Bamse ignited a huge outpouring of grief. Businesses closed for his funeral, and some eight hundred children lined the route to his grave. He was buried near the sea, facing Norway.

Sixty-two years later, on the July 22, 2006, anniversary of his death, Bamse was awarded a prestigious Gold Medal from Britain's People's Dispensary for Sick Animals (PDSA) for his

wartime service. That same year, a bronze statue of the great Saint Bernard was unveiled in Montrose to serve as a living tribute to Norway's most-loved dog.

JUDY

THE DOG WHO BECAME A PRISONER OF WAR

Of all the world's canines of distinction, an English pointer named Judy probably owns the most dubious honor. The poor dog, born in 1936 in Shanghai, spent the balance of World War II in a squalid Japanese prison camp. While there, she became the only canine in the entire conflict to be officially registered as a prisoner of war.

At the beginning of the struggle she enjoyed a decidedly loftier status as the mascot of the British warship HMS *Grasshopper*. But the ship was sunk by Japanese torpedoes in 1942, marooning the survivors, Judy included, on an island off Sumatra. The dog sniffed out sources of fresh water for her thirsty comrades, her first display of the resourcefulness that would make her a hero. Unfortunately, she couldn't prevent the crew's capture by Japanese troops and their subsequent shipment to a prison camp.

Judy did, however, go along to the camp, smuggled inside a seaman's sack. Life for the prisoners was brutal, but the noble canine did what she could, often at great personal risk, to help the men around her. Fellow prisoner Frank Williams shared his meager rations with Judy, and in exchange she became his trusted friend, doing her best to distract the sadistic Japanese guards when they seemed bent on attacking him and the other prisoners. Eventually Williams convinced the camp commandant to register her as an official prisoner—serial number POW81A.

The camp's guards tried repeatedly to shoot Judy, but they weren't the only danger she faced. In addition to taking a couple of bullet wounds, she survived fights with alligators, wild dogs, and even a Sumatran tiger before finally being liberated, along with her human camp mates, at the war's end in 1945. Williams brought Judy back to England, where she was awarded the People's Dispensary for Sick Animals (PDSA) Dickin Medal, England's highest honor for animal valor. Judy got another reward as well—the chance to spend the rest of her life with her beloved Frank Williams. The noble dog expired in 1950 in the African nation of Tanzania, where Williams had taken a job. A stone memorial marks her grave, and her Dickin Medal and the custom collar from which it hung now reside in London's Imperial War Museum.

TANG

THE DOG WHO SAVED AN ENTIRE SHIP

For centuries gigantic, coal-black Newfoundlands have served as lifeguards on beaches and aboard ships. Their waterproof coats and webbed toes make them excellent swimmers, and their size (more than one hundred pounds [45 kg]), strength, and endurance allow them to plow through pounding surf, grab foundering humans in their jaws, and haul them back safely to land.

These heroic guardians have saved thousands of lives. But even in such celebrated company, the deeds of one canine stalwart stand out. Tang, the ship's dog of the coastal steamer SS *Ethie*, didn't save just one soul from a watery grave—he saved every single person on his vessel.

Just before Christmas of 1919, the *Ethie* departed Port Saunders, Newfoundland, for St. John's Harbor. A violent storm tossed the ship onto the rocks, seemingly dooming its ninety-two passengers and crew. Their only chance was to get a line to rescuers on shore and use it to haul everyone to safety before the storm pounded the hapless vessel apart.

But someone would have to physically carry the line through half a mile (805 m) of freezing, storm-tossed chop to reach the beach. The feat was plainly beyond the physical capabilities of even the hardiest members of the crew. All save for one.

According to contemporary accounts, the ship's dog, Tang, was more than up to the job. Taking the end of the lifesaving rope in his mouth, he reportedly plunged into the dark, churning sea and dog-paddled his way to the coast, where he handed over the line to waiting rescuers. Once it was secured, the rescue team rigged a pulley system and sent a chair out to the *Ethie*. One by one, the passengers, the crew, and finally the captain were hauled to shore.

The dog's achievement made him a Canadian national hero. He was even awarded a medal by the famous insurance company Lloyds of London. Thanks to Tang, a disaster that easily could have claimed dozens of lives became a mere footnote in maritime history. Today the rusting remains of the ill-starred ship can still be seen on the Newfoundland coast—a silent testament both to the power of the sea and to the indomitable will of a heroic canine.

CHIPS

THE MOST-DECORATED WAR DOG OF WORLD WAR II

Canines served on all fronts during World War II, but few as effectively as an innocuous-looking German shepherd/husky/collie mix named Chips. Donated to the war effort by his master, Edward J. Wren of Pleasantville, New York, Chips was trained as a sentry dog and assigned to the 3rd Infantry Division. During the war he served in eight separate campaigns that took him through North Africa, Sicily, Italy, France, and Germany.

On July 10, 1943, Chips made his mark in history. During the invasion of Sicily, his unit was pinned down by a machine gun nest. Enraged, Chips charged the gun emplacement and, in spite of taking several bullets, gave its occupants a savage mauling that forced their surrender.

His valor earned Chips a meeting with Allied supreme commander Dwight D. Eisenhower, as well as a Silver Star and Purple Heart. The U.S. Army later revoked both awards, fearing that giving them to a dog was an affront to human soldiers. Chips didn't complain, but it's doubtful that the men in his unit, some of whom wouldn't have survived the war without his vigilance, agreed.

PERITAS

THE DOG WHO SAVED ALEXANDER THE GREAT

None of history's great military commanders can match the achievements of Alexander the Great. Born in the year 356 BCE in the tiny nation of Macedon, he led its miniscule army on an epic mission of global conquest, forging the largest empire the world had yet seen before dying at age thirty-two.

His greatest accomplishment was subduing the Persian Empire, the ancient world's only superpower. At the battle of Gaugamela, Alexander routed the Persians by personally leading a cavalry charge into their ranks, straight at their king, Darius. This extremely risky move won him eternal glory—though it could just as easily have cost him his life. It is said that at one point during the onslaught, a war elephant charged Alexander, who was caught by surprise and almost trampled. But at the last moment his huge dog, Peritas, charged the elephant, bit its lower lip, and hung on. The attack gave Alexander just enough time to escape.

Peritas wasn't as lucky. After the battle the Macedonians recovered his body and gave the dog a state funeral. Alexander named a city after the dog, to whom he owed his life and his empire.

SMOKIE

THE LITTLEST WAR DOG

Smokie, a Yorkshire terrier weighing in at just four pounds (2 kg), was the smallest pooch—probably the smallest *anything*—to serve in the Pacific during World War II.

Her military career began when an American GI found her, abandoned, in a foxhole on the island of New Guinea. Her savior gave her to another soldier, who sold her to a member of the U.S. Army Air Force, William A. Wynne, for the equivalent of about $6.50. Smokie stuck with Wynne from then on, flying twelve combat missions with the Air Force's 26th Photo Reconnaissance Squadron. During the battle for the Philippines, she even dragged a communications cable seventy feet (21 m) through an eight-inch-wide (20 cm) pipe under an airplane runway.

After *Yank* magazine called Smokie "the best mascot in the South Pacific," the tiny soldier started making morale visits to hospitals. She continued cheering up sick vets until her death in 1957. Today a monument to this little dog's towering achievements stands in Cleveland.

BARRY

THE GREATEST OF ALL SAINT BERNARDS

For hundreds of years, monks have manned a traveler's way station in the forbidding 8,100-foot-high Great Saint Bernard Pass, a treacherous Alpine trail that tenuously links Italy to Switzerland. Established in the eleventh century by Bernard de Menthon, the inhabitants of the monastery looked out for travelers who got into trouble while trying to negotiate the often-frozen, usually snow-clogged, and always avalanche-prone route. During the eighteenth century the monks developed a special corps of hulking mountain dogs to assist them—a breed we know today as the Saint Bernard. Over the years these dogs saved the lives of some two thousand travelers, digging them out of avalanches or guiding them safely through raging blizzards.

But the big, shaggy canines didn't always go by their present name. Thanks to the exploits of one particular guardian—perhaps the most famous rescue canine of all time—the breed was once nicknamed the Barry Dog.

The celebrated Barry worked at the high mountain pass from 1800 to 1810, saving a reported forty travelers from icy deaths. Interestingly, legend holds that the heroic dog died at the hands of his forty-first attempted rescue—a soldier, lost in a blinding snowstorm, who stabbed the huge creature approaching him, thinking he was a wolf. There is even a prominent monument raised to Barry's memory in Paris that bears the inscription, "He saved the lives of 40 persons. He was killed by the 41st."

Happily, that tale is a myth. In truth, Barry was taken to the Swiss capital of Berne in 1810, where he spent two years in leisurely retirement before passing peacefully at the age of fourteen. Barry's remains are still displayed at the main entrance of Berne's Natural History Museum. His lithe, muscular body and short hair don't look much like the ideal Saint Bernard show dog of today. But that's to be expected. In his day, dogs in his line of work were judged by what they could do, rather than how they looked.

The ancient way station at Saint Bernard continues to honor its most famous guardian's memory by always keeping one dog in the kennel named Barry. And the more "exciting" version of Barry's death—that he was killed by a man he wanted to rescue—refuses to be laid to rest.

JACK

THE ARMY DOG WHO WAS JUST AS VALUABLE AS A HUMAN

During the American Civil War, a brown-and-white bull terrier named Jack served as mascot for the 102nd Pennsylvania Infantry. The faithful dog followed his unit through many bloody battles, including Spotsylvania and the siege of Petersburg. His human comrades in arms claimed that Jack only obeyed commands from men in his particular unit and could understand the different bugle calls used to rally the troops. During engagements Jack selflessly exposed himself to enemy fire, and after battles he would track down his regiment's injured and wounded and summon help.

He may have exposed himself a bit too much to enemy guns. He was seriously wounded during one battle and barely escaped death, and Confederate soldiers twice captured him. Incredibly, when he was taken the second time, his Union companions offered to exchange a human prisoner to get him back. The opposition agreed to the deal, and a Confederate infantryman was duly traded for the dog. To honor his achievements, the men of the 102nd gave Jack a silver collar to wear, but shortly thereafter he vanished. His heartbroken soldier friends assumed he was probably stolen, right along with his flashy new neckpiece.

FLOSSIE

THE OWNER OF THE WORLD'S MOST EXPENSIVE DOG HOUSE

All dogs deserve rewards for good behavior. But when their conduct is truly exemplary—and their grateful owners are really, really wealthy—the payoff may be far more substantial than a Milk Bone or a pat on the head.

Consider the rags-to-riches story of Flossie, a Labrador retriever mixed breed who spent her early years as a stray, roaming the streets of Pasadena, California. Then one fortuitous day, she ran into actress Drew Barrymore. Barrymore fell in love with the gigantic yellow mutt and took her to live with her in her Beverly Hills home.

But what began as a Cinderella story soon turned into an adventure tale. On the night of February 18, 2001, Barrymore and her then-fiancé Tom Green were awakened at 3 A.M. as Flossie made a huge racket outside their master suite. She "literally banged on their bedroom door," the couple's spokesperson told the Associated Press. "Flossie was really the main alert that there was a fire."

The inferno took sixty Los Angeles Fire Department firefighters more than an hour to extinguish. It consumed Barrymore's 3,500-square-foot (325 sq m) abode, causing about $700,000 in damage. But things could have been much worse. If Flossie hadn't switched into "Lassie mode" and saved the day, the home's human occupants might not have awakened in time to escape. Thanks to their four-legged smoke alarm, Barrymore and Green got out, as did Flossie and the couple's two other dogs. "We're great," Barrymore told reporters at the scene.

"Other than the fact that the home burned down," Green added.

Flossie got her reward about two years later, after the fire-gutted house was restored to its former grandeur. Barrymore decided to show her appreciation for her furry friend and personal savior by giving the canine legal title to the newly renovated, $3-million domicile. "Drew and Tom love that dog more than anything in the world," a family friend told the Associated Press. "They want to know she'll always have a roof over her head." Along with indoor plumbing, central heating, and a wait staff, of course.

GINNY

THE DOG WHO BECAME AN HONORARY CAT

In theory, canines are the mortal enemies of cats. But the true nature of their relationship is far more complicated. While the typical beagle or Jack Russell terrier may enjoy pursuing a hapless feline around its front yard, not all dogs see cats as annoyances or opponents to bully. Some actually see them as friends.

The most famous of these canine cat lovers was a mixed-breed dog from New York named Ginny. Called by some the "Mother Teresa of cats," she saved roughly nine hundred of them from death, disease, and starvation during her seventeen-year life.

Her story began when she was adopted from a Long Beach, New York, shelter by construction worker Philip Gonzalez. Though he originally wanted to get a Doberman pinscher, the shaggy, decidedly odd-looking schnauzer/Siberian husky cross caught his eye—and won his heart. As it turned out, Ginny's looks weren't the only thing unusual about her. She loved cats, and cats loved her, too. She adored them so much that she started seeking out felines in distress. "I didn't train her," Gonzalez told the Associated Press. "Ginny was just magical in a way. . . . She just had this knack of knowing when a cat was in trouble."

During one of her first rescues, Ginny found five kittens trapped in a pipe at a construction site. She came to the aid of cats in Dumpsters, alleyways, and abandoned cars. Once she even found a kitten at the bottom of a box of broken glass. Gonzalez was soon caring (and paying) for an endless procession of foundling felines. But Ginny helped with finances, too—she served as the inspiration for two best-selling books, *The Dog Who Rescues Cats* and *The Blessing of the Animals*.

Ginny pursued her unique calling until her death on August 25, 2005. After her passing she was eulogized at the prestigious Westchester Cat Show—the same show that had awarded her with an unprecedented honor in 1998, when the dog who loved felines was named Cat of the Year.

OTHER CANINES OF DISTINCTION

MANCS: A Hungarian earthquake rescue dog who gained worldwide fame in 1999 for finding a three-year-old Turkish girl trapped for eighty-two hours under a collapsed building.

JUST NUISANCE: A Great Dane who, in August 1939, became the only canine to offically enlist in Britain's Royal Navy. A fixture at the Simon's Town Naval Base near Cape Town, South Africa, he made a habit of riding trains with his sailor friends. When rail authorities complained, base officials enrolled him in the Navy—because sailors could take the trains for free.

LA DIABLE: The French dog who wore a false fur coat to smuggle contraband across the border during the French Revolution.

SIR PEERS LEGH'S MASTIFF: A female war dog who protected her master for hours after he was wounded during the Battle of Agincourt. Her offspring helped form the modern mastiff breed.

BRIAN: A German shepherd attached to Great Britain's 13th Battalion Airborne Division, he parachuted into Normandy with his unit at the start of D-day.